Loving your Sensitive Self

A Guide to
Managing and Protecting
Your Energy

Rachel Scoltock

First published 2010 for Rachel Scoltock

Cover design: Ina Kuehfuss - Inawonderworld Design - www.inawonderworld.com

Copyright © Rachel Scoltock 2010

All rights reserved. No part of this publication may be reproduced or transmitted in any form or by any means, electronic or mechanical, including photocopying, recording or by any information storage and retrieval system, without the prior permission in writing from the author, publisher and copyright holders.

National Library of Australia Cataloguing-in-Publication entry
Author: Scoltock, Rachel.
Title: Loving your sensitive self : a guide to managing and protecting your energy / Rachel Scoltock.
Edition: 1st ed.
ISBN: 9781920681548 (pbk.)
Subjects: Healers.
Mental healing.
Naturopathy.
Dewey Number: 615.852

I dedicate this to you with the prayer that through embracing and nurturing your sensitive gifts you will discover and experience the divine being that you truly are.

Rachel Scoltock

is an angel medium, author and teacher. An expert in angels and energy medicine, Rachel offers private sessions, readings and classes to heal and transform your life.

You can connect with Rachel through her website

rachelscoltock.com

or by writing to

rachel@rachelscoltock.com

Contents

Acknowledgements	8
Foreword	9

Chapter 1

What this book is about	11
What is sensitivity?	13
A journey from insensitive to sensitive	14
Sensitive Indigenous peoples	16
Overriding sensitivity	18
My experiences as a sensitive	21
How it feels to be sensitive	23
Are you a sensitive?	25
The sensitive guidance system	29
The psychic connection	33
Sensitive children	34
Wanting to go home	36
The purpose of sensitivity	37

Chapter 2

Angels	39
Healing with angels	40
Archangels	42
Angel invocation	44
How to tell that angels are around	45
Angels and the Law of Attraction	47
How Angel Healing works	48

Chapter 3

What is energy?	53
The energy of emotions	55
How emotional energy effects a sensitive	56
Entrainment	57
Energy to fuel your life	58
Managing your aura	60
Unhealthy ways to replenish energy	64
A healthier way to find energy	66
How your energy can leak	67
Abundance and your energy	72

Chapter 4
How to heal without being drained	74
Permission to heal	76
Allowing yourself to receive	76
Managing energetic intrusions	78
The energy of locations	79
Emotional energy	80
Addictions	83
Healing addictions	86
Toxins, diet and the sensitive person	86

Chapter 5
Clearing, Grounding and Protecting your energy	91
Energy clearing	93
Chakra clearing with the Mermaids	95
Grounding your energy	100
Quick fixes for when you feel ungrounded	103
Shielding	104
Quick fixes for protecting your energy	109

Chapter 6
The other side of the fence: Respecting people's energy	111
Energetic sticky beaks	112
A shielding visualisation to protect against probing energy	113
Ties	114
Signs that you may have ties	118
How to cut ties	119
Releasing negativity and fear	121
Managing resentment and psychic attack from other people	123
How to prevent sending psychic attack	126
A note on swearing and cursing	127
Affirmations	128

Chapter 7
Bringing it all together	134

Glossary	136

Acknowledgements

Much of this information has come via my angelic guides to whom I am deeply grateful; I am also thankful to the clients who shared their stories for this book and whom I have been honoured to work with on their journeys.

Foreword

I always knew I was sensitive but until a few years ago, it seemed I was alone with my tendency to feel overwhelmed in crowded places, drained by an interaction with a friend or unwell in antique shops. I was often told that I was 'over sensitive' when I reacted with extreme emotion that corresponded to the feelings of the people around me. I felt sick in negative environments; I could feel the physical pain of others; I felt horribly drained in my work as a public servant, and although I wanted to help people, their sad stories exhausted me. I was confused. I struggled with rollercoaster energy and emotions, and felt very stuck.

Today, as a healer, my sensitivity is the channel through which I receive intuitive information about my clients from their energy and spiritual guides. Whether I am giving a reading, healing or channeling, my physical and emotional feelings blend with and complement my work. What seemed to be an affliction is actually a gift. I no longer feel drained when encountering someone's pain; in fact, the signals I receive are often accompanied with insight and solutions.

I am able to do this because I have learned and implemented some very simple techniques in order to protect and manage my sensitivity and my own energy field. This information works just as well for everyone.

I have also discovered that I am far from alone. An ever-increasing number of my clients are suffering with sensitivity in varying degrees. The younger clientele in particular are highly sensitive to foods, chemicals and the emotions of others. I began to notice that many clients needed to know how to protect and manage their energy in the ways that I had learned.

I printed an information sheet and soon I was receiving more and more requests for it. Everyone who read and used the methods reported an almost instant improvement in how they were feeling. They began to make positive changes to their lives, because they had stronger boundaries and were feeling less victimised and drained. Confusion and indecision lifted to reveal intuitive clarity. Of course, not every sensitive chooses to work as a healer; everyone has his or her own personal life path to discover. Tuning into your sensitivity and creating stronger energetic boundaries makes it easier to find that path.

Through working with sensitive clients and facilitating the healing of their unique challenges, as well as my own, I have learned and developed the techniques and insights that make up this book.

Chapter 1

What this book is about

This book offers a positive and insightful perspective to sensitivity and energy. It provides practical and easy to use methods to overcome the difficult aspects of being a deeply sensitive person in a seemingly insensitive world.

The spiritual healing and visualisation techniques will work to effortlessly clear protect and centre your sensitive energy. These methods will act as a barrier to outside energy, and help you to remain centred, clear and energised.

You will discover how your personal energy field or aura behaves and how to consciously manage it to protect and strengthen you on all levels. You will learn to prevent your unconscious self-sabotaging behaviours and transform them to positively attract what you do want at an energetic level. You can even use these methods to finally heal addictions and other unhealthy behaviours. With the help of this information, your gift of sensitivity can be nurtured and developed to become a reliable intuitive guidance tool for yourself and others. Sensitivity is a wonderful healing gift; available to anyone, to be used for the good of all and recognised as an integral part of healing our planet.

All people are sensitive by nature but there are many adults and children who are deeply sensitive and feel that the only solution is to harden to the so-called realities of life or withdraw completely. Sensitive people constantly struggle with their physical and emotional responses to the world around them; their environments, the foods they eat and the people they encounter. To a sensitive negative energy or toxins can be unbearable but seemingly impossible to avoid. As a result, many sensitive people suffer with health issues, emotional struggles, relationship and career problems that could easily be avoided and overcome with awareness and the knowledge of how to clear and protect their energy.

Sensitive's are often intuitive, even psychic and are able to detect spiritual beings, feelings and intuitive messages from the energy of the people and places around them.

The very essence of everything in our world is energy; the most solid material objects are made up of dancing energy particles. We are vibrational energy, as are our thoughts, emotions and words. All energy can be sensed by, and absorbed into, our own physical bodies. Our reactions to energy depend upon whether it is charged with positive or negative vibrations and how sensitive we are to it. Once absorbed, negative or toxic energy can wreak havoc on a sensitive person leading to confusion, fatigue and even illness. Most people do not relate these health or emotional issues to energy sensitivity and therefore do not realise how easily they can be overcome.

Through the healing described in the following chapters, you will learn to clear, ground and protect yourself and bring your energy vibration into alignment with everything you want. You will be able to achieve clarity about what you do and do not want and make great decisions. You will start to walk your life path with confidence and purpose and attract abundance in the form of opportunities, people and items that are in alignment with what you want and your purpose.

What is sensitivity?

You have a higher self; a wise being inside of you, which knows everything about you and what you need. It constantly communicates with you through your thoughts, feelings, emotions and body. If you choose to listen to and follow this being's advice, you can be at optimum health and wellbeing in every aspect of your life. All beings are sensitive by nature. Everyone on the planet has the ability to develop their sensitivity and understand energy to improve their lives.

Sensitivity means that you detect through all of your senses what is happening within and around you. In other words, you can sense whether something is good or bad through the reactions of your body, your senses, your emotions and your intuition.

Sensitivity is most commonly experienced in response to the foods and beverages that you ingest, information that you read, hear, see and absorb from people, television, the Internet and other media, frequencies in the atmosphere, emotions, electro-magnetic energy, pollutants in cleaning products, pesticides, medicines and drugs.

All of these have an affect your sensitive body in varying degrees and may manifest as an allergy, food intolerance, emotional imbalance, disease or disorder.

You may find you have a strong sensitivity to the energy and emotions of other people. This is type of sensitivity is called empathy. The energy of others can have an enormous effect on your emotions, physical health and vitality. As an empathic, it is important to become aware and learn how to manage this form of sensitivity to be able to discern your own emotions from those of others.

You may also find that you are receiving information from the spiritual realms from angels, deceased loved ones, spirit guides and past lives, or even lower energies such as entities. You definitely have the ability to tune into these realms if you choose. Psychic sensitivity without awareness can be compared to an untuned radio. You receive a great deal of information but it is often very fuzzy and confusing!

The ability to tune into and absorb emotions and energy from people, places and spirits is a psychic gift of empathy and healing but without awareness it can have a crippling effect on the way you feel. Depending on your level of sensitivity, the negative energy absorbed from a depressed or angry person can leave you feeling: heavy, depressed, angry, ill, tired, emotional, and even experiencing physical pain.

Many sensitives are natural counsellors and healers. If this sounds like you, you will regularly encounter sad and challenged people who feel compelled to share their problems with you, you will also feel compelled to care for and heal others. A build up of the toxic energy received from people releasing their pain, can lead physical and emotional blockages. This is until you become aware of how to release and transmute the negative energy that you have absorbed from the other person.

A journey from Insensitive to Sensitive

Sensitivity is a natural part of human nature. Desensitisation has occurred with the onset of our civilised world. Technology, a strive for prosperity and mass production has taken human lifestyle away from the natural world and surrounded us with materialism, manmade replacements, false lighting, chemicals and technology based entertainment and work practices.

Part of our journey in life is to become our natural authentic sensitive selves, to act, speak and live according to our true nature. Our authentic selves are loving, compassionate, peaceful, abundant and sensitive.

When we act according to the authentic self, we honour our true needs and emotions, and through doing this we truly live according to higher will and fulfil our utmost potential.

In this space of love and happiness, we easily respect our selves, our planet, everything, and everyone on it and everything naturally and beautifully falls into place.

The challenge for each of us is to break through the barriers, which have desensitised our authentic voice so that we can clearly hear our higher selves, our soul, and the voice of the divine. The test is to follow that voice, to dare to rise to the calling of the soul. It is only then that we can honestly live in love, peace, harmony and happiness.

The unnatural lifestyles that many people lead are largely the result of misinformation and a lack of knowledge. We are often unaware that we regularly ingest and absorb toxic ingredients that damage the body and mind, creating disease, addictions, emotional stress, poor concentration and disharmony. These unnatural behaviours can desensitise and block our sensitive systems so it becomes harder to listen to our true self.

Intuition and sensitivity are not traits that are generally highly valued in mainstream society — at least not as valued as commerciality, competition, and indifference. We are taught the ego view, that it is a 'dog eat dog' world and we have to 'fight' to get our share, that there is 'not enough to go around'. These fearful scenarios cause us to create the very things we fear through our focus upon them. This is the Law of Attraction.

We need natural light and fresh air to survive; yet, so many people work all day in buildings that starve their bodies of the elements of nature necessary to keep healthy. We need fresh clean water and life giving fruit and vegetables. Yet many Western diets are filled with processed, chemical laden foods and drinks and many people are dehydrated. Stressful situations traumatise and harm the body, mind and spirit, as do the damaging substances that are often used to cope with the stress: cigarettes, alcohol, medication and caffeine. We disassociate from our true feelings, by using alcohol and drugs, overwork, television, computer games and junk food.

Intuition is rarely used to connect to a higher source for guidance and protection. We seldom connect with nature and have lost touch with how to respond to the natural ebb and flow of our energy. We have forgotten that we need these things to survive and remain in balance.

We behave negatively because we have desensitised, we cannot and do not hear or feel the truth of our actions often until it is too late. Many negative conditions can be avoided just by tuning into our sensitive bodies and feelings. So much suffering, disease and conflict could be eliminated if humanity was to begin to live according to their authentic higher will rather than the desensitised ego.

The good news is that humanity is gradually waking up. This change in attitude is occurring one person at a time, with each sensitive person who chooses to honour his or her authentic self.

Sensitive Indigenous peoples

The Indigenous peoples of the world lived, and still live, with sensitivity and in tune to nature and their true selves.

The Australian Indigenous people, just like the Native American people and other indigenous cultures, traditionally live close to nature and in balance with it. They recognise themselves as a part of nature and traditionally use only what they need, giving thanks through ceremony and ritual for their abundance. They communicate with the spirit world, nature and the divine and live according to the laws of these realms so as not to upset the delicate balance of life. They have medicines, healing, food, warmth, spirituality, education, law, entertainment, work and family – everything they need and desire.

They are sensitive to themselves and the environment they live in. They are sensitive to spirit- their ancestors, the spirits of nature and their Gods, and creator spirits.

Eventually as their lands were colonised, these sensitive peoples had other less sensitive societies impose their diets and habits upon them. There was a dramatic reaction to the new settlers who brought with them disease, ideas, foods and alcohol. They often forced Indigenous peoples to live according to their rules – inside buildings, apart from nature, away from families, the lands and hunting and gathering grounds of their ancestors.

These things were done because of the quest for land that many modern societies felt was necessary for economic and political survival and because they felt they were morally or religiously 'right'. These actions had a devastating effect, the results of which can still be seen today. Amongst Indigenous peoples there are dramatically higher mortality rates, a high incidence of diabetes and other issues associated with eating processed foods, a much reduced population, grief, abuse and addiction. This list is characteristic of many Indigenous peoples across the globe. However, disease, abuse and addiction occur in all human societies, not solely indigenous ones.

What sets the Indigenous statistics apart is that Indigenous people were only introduced to the behaviours relatively recently; before this time they were living peacefully and successfully with nature without some of these problems. The negative effects that are now manifesting show the shock of the elements of a desensitised society upon a more sensitive culture.

We are all one peoples and suffering the same problems in varying degrees. For most societies toxic behaviours have been around for a longer time and this has caused a hardening against the barrage of unhealthy influences: a desensitisation.

The solution is to get back in touch with our true selves; to listen and respond to the needs of our bodies, mind and emotions and to speak our truths and honour every living being, beginning with us, by listening to and honouring our sensitivity.

Humanity is, in essence, sensitive and loving. Any ability to perform negative acts originates from living a toxic, insensitive lifestyle.

In bringing to light these issues, it is not my intention to create resentment or anger towards the past. It is important to release ego thoughts such as guilt, judgement and fear about events that happened or are happening. Such thoughts only add to the illusion of fear and perpetrate the feeling that people are powerless victims. This is false and does nothing to help or heal anyone.

To heal the past and present, hold loving thoughts and ask your guides to help you to release all fear and resentment. Bless the past and take from it the lessons. In this case, the lesson is about living sensitively whilst acting and speaking in loving ways. Forgiveness is a powerful tool that allows you to release harsh energy and live your life with freedom and love.

Overriding sensitivity

You cannot switch off your sensitivity no matter how hard you try. Even though you may feel overwhelmed with what seems like a bombardment of incoming energy. It is normal to want to numb your sensitivity, to ignore or override it to the point that you do not even hear or feel the reactions in your body and emotions, especially if they are painful. This comes with the misguided thought that you cannot control outside circumstances so you might as well try to be like everyone else and fit in. The only way seems to be to desensitise.

The truth is that you cannot control this situation but you can learn ways to manage and protect your sensitive energy, which will empower you and preserve your health and allow you to be yourself.

When you nurture your sensitivity it will help you to have clear boundaries and make good, positive decisions. When you try to desensitise you actually end up with more pain and it takes longer to learn your life lessons.

You may be receiving signals from your senses which you do not understand or know how to control. The truth is that the reactions have a message for you. If this inner wisdom is ignored, it will increase until it becomes physical or emotional pain as attempts at desensitisation numb the more subtle voice of the intuition.

For instance, a person might feel uncomfortable or unwell when they eat sugary foods but crave them for the energy boost. The craving and belief that the sugar will create energy has replaced the intuitive guidance that this is not a healthy choice. Initially the intuition may guide us to think that sugar is unhealthy; it may speak through the emotions with guilt or another negative feeling.

When these signs are ignored, the intuition will attempt to talk through the physical feelings. If these are ignored, the negative reaction, such as headaches or depression, can become really painful. The pain is the intuitions' way of getting you to address the imbalanced behaviour.

In the case of sugar, this person might ignore the sugary highs and lows or headaches and eventually develop an extreme 'sign' such as diabetes, obesity or tooth cavities that signal the dire need to give up the sugar.

To honour your sensitivity means that you do not ignore pain and signals in or around you. It means being in tune with your whole self and listening to your higher self to make decisions. Your higher self is your true self who is always connected to God; it will never lie to you.

Pain is always a sign that something is imbalanced.

You can learn from pain, but it is a slow process, especially as it has to seep through the thick skin created by habitual desensitisation. Sometimes it is difficult to undo the effects that pain has created; there are many stories of people turning their lives around after a shocking and painful situation has brought them to a realisation about their thoughts or behaviour. Pain is not the only way to learn our growth lessons we can learn from loving situations much more quickly and as effectively if we choose!

Your intuition is always talking to you, the longer it is ignored the stronger, and more painful the signal will be. It usually begins with gentle nudges, gradually increasing until you can no longer ignore it. I call this the 'Universal kick up the butt'. By the time a signal has increased to the 'kick up the butt' stage it will manifest as mental, emotional or physical pain, a crisis or disease.

Pain is the higher self's way of firmly and finally calling our attention to a toxic behaviour, belief or action, leaving us with a signal that cannot be ignored. These situations often require a complete turn around of attitude and lifestyle. You can begin loving yourself by listening to your wise sensitive energy. This way you learn from love rather than pain and avoid a painful kick up the butt!

We tend to ignore early signals because consuming and absorbing toxins can dull our senses. Intuition is all but drowned out by pollutants, sugar, alcohol, negative media, mind chatter, and busyness. It is easy to become distracted by entertainment, shopping, electronic communication and worry.

Media marketing continually pushes us to do more, want more, and get more for our happiness. Most people are accustomed to listening to any other authority than their inner selves. It does not have to be this way. Everything can change with a little knowledge and awareness and a willingness to try something new.

To begin clearing away pain and confusion, honour your true sensitive nature and listen to your physical, emotional and spiritual signals. A good way to start is to spend a few moments alone each day in quiet contemplation. Meditation, a morning walk or even journaling can quiet the mind and allow your inner self to be heard.

This awareness will also bring a beautiful divine connection if you wish. As you understand that consciousness and all the guidance you need comes not from outside yourself but within where it has always been!

My experiences as a Sensitive

Like many sensitive people, I initially had a very difficult time in my relationships and working life. I found negativity in other people, institutions and buildings overwhelming at times and suffered emotional and physical symptoms such as depression, unexplained nausea, stomach pains and sinus troubles.

I began to notice that these symptoms stopped when I changed jobs, homes or ended certain relationships. I realised that I had been ignoring these symptoms or looking for unrelated reasons for them until they had become unbearable. I had tried to persevere with unpleasant circumstances because I thought I had to. I thought myself over sensitive and tried to change myself to fit in. To exacerbate this belief I was constantly told I was too sensitive and over emotional. This led me to believe that I was in someway wrong.

I constantly overrode my intuition in favour of what I thought I should do often to please others. I became depressed and lacked in real direction. Over time I began to discover that it was impossible to override my feelings, no matter how hard I tried, because it was physically harming me. The longer I stayed in uncomfortable situations the sicker I became; I definitely was not finding happiness.

From an early age, I attracted many people who wanted to

share their problems with me. I mostly enjoyed this role as I had a knack for insight and being able to say the right thing at the right moment. I had an inner desire to help and to heal. However, I found that counselling and listening could leave me exhausted, and feeling low. My compassion seemed to work against me!

I felt my best when I was close to nature, with gentle people or animals; I felt the worst in crowds or around heavy energy of drugs, alcohol or anger. I chose to spend a lot of time alone without any real understanding how energy and emotions were affecting me.

It was through my studies as a healer that I finally discovered that my sensitivity was meaningful and a part of my life purpose.

I learned that there were names for my 'problem': clairsentient, empathic or sensitive, and that my physical and emotional symptoms were actually intuitive messages about myself and other people. In fact some of the advice I was giving came directly from my intuition! I suddenly realised how unnecessary and counterproductive it had been to try to turn these signals off!

Eventually, I learned how to utilise my sensitivity in my healing work and manage it in my own life. I discovered how to protect my energy and cleanse away the debris of other people's emotions. With a few life style adjustments, I am finally free of debilitating symptoms and confusion.

What had seemed to be a liability became an empowering gift of intuition and healing and an important key to my life purpose!

I now clearly feel and hear my own inner voice, the voices of my angels and guides, and I can psychically tune into the energy of my clients at will, to discover what messages their bodies and angels have for them. I can do all of this without having to suffer the draining and debilitating effects that I had suffered for so long. From my experiences, I now understand that there is a great need for this information to become more widely available: to help more sensitive people to learn the basics about managing energy. This knowledge is empowering and transformative — I have experienced it in my own life and seen it working through the lives of my clients. I always feel so grateful to be an intermediary for these transformations.

How it feels to be Sensitive

As a sensitive person, you can waiver between feeling vulnerably fragile and insightfully perceptive.

Which is the truth: are you thin skinned or intuitive? Is your sensitivity a positive or a negative trait? The answer is both, until you learn to manage and protect your sensitive energy so that it becomes a positive and treasured part of your life.

You are sensitive because you experience the world through your feelings and other senses more strongly than other people; your perception is heightened and everything is felt very deeply.

You can regularly feel overwhelmed, fatigued, drained and unsettled. Energy that you sense from within and around you can create all sorts of reactions in your body and emotions. It can be difficult to know how to manage or interpret these feelings. Sometimes it can just be difficult to get through an ordinary day!

The good news is that you can learn how to manage your sensitivity to outside energy in such a way that your life becomes easier, clearer and has more direction. You will still feel and sense the world around you but you will not take on the associated energy and if you do you will know how to easily clear it. You will learn that you have a wise internal guidance system that teaches you every moment what is good for your wellbeing and can direct you towards a happier, healthier and more meaningful life experience.

Your sensitivity has a real purpose and is a special ability rather than a liability. As you honour this gift, it can act as your powerful and reliable guide. You will gain life direction, access to spiritual guidance, profound insight and the steps to healing yourself.

You will increase your spiritual knowledge and intuition as you learn about your personal energy field and how the energy of the world affects and interacts with you. You will learn ways to protect this energy field so that you do not absorb outside energy and lose your own precious life force.

As a result, you will find that you have more health and vitality to enjoy your life, you will be clearer headed and more confident to make decisions, you will find that you begin to attract more positive experiences and relationships.

The methods included in this book will help you to develop and heighten your intuitive abilities, teach how to heal your life via your auric field, help you to heal addictions and connect to an unfailing source of energy and vitality.

Once adopted, these practices will help you know how it feels to live freely without being caught up with the effects of outside influences on your receptive energies. Healing, manifesting and adopting the universal spiritual principles such as the Law of Attraction will become effortless.

Through learning what it means to be spiritually sensitive you can overcome the difficulties and unique traits that all sensitive people can experience.

You will find references to divine Angels scattered throughout this book with guidance to connecting with these powerful spiritual guides and inviting them to the healing processes. I work very closely with angels in my healing practice and much of the information that inspired this book was given to me by them, supported with testimonials and case studies gathered through my own experiences.

Are you a Sensitive?

Many sensitive people do not understand what is happening and tend to believe that something is wrong with them. When I tell a client they are a sensitive, they are often relieved and excited to discover that they are not at fault and that what they are dealing with is easy to correct and manage. Sensitive people tend to have similar characteristics that can seem to make their situation worse but are actually clues to their life's purpose and the gifts that they possess. All sensitives are born with a unique set of tools; it is just that someone forgot to give them the manual!

Here are some questions to help you define whether you are a sensitive:

- Do you regularly experience strong reactions and a high sensitivity to anger and other emotions in people?

- Do you have intolerances, allergies or negative reactions to certain foods and beverages, such as processed, unnatural foods or those high in sugar or caffeine?

- Do you react to chemicals in cleaning products and other items?

- Do you get headaches or tiredness from computers or false lighting?

- Have you felt overwhelmed or ill in busy places such as shopping centres, markets or airports?

- Do you feel drained, sad or elated depending on the energy of the people that you interact with?

- Can you sense the emotional or physical symptoms of others in your own body?

- Do you cry easily?

- Do you experience regular déjà vu, goose bumps and other bodily reactions without fully understanding why?

- Have you experienced feeling physically or emotionally unwell in certain buildings, areas or when you are with certain people?

- Do you have a tendency to avoid certain situations or people?

- Do you yearn to spend time alone?

- Do you regularly feel fatigued or emotional without knowing why?

- Have you sensed 'vibes' from animals, locations, spiritual beings or inanimate items?

- Do you have quiet intuitive nudges about people that often turn out to be correct?

- Do you find it challenging to decipher between your thoughts, fear and intuitive guidance?

- Do people tend to share their problems and life stories with you?

- Are children and animals attracted to you and visa versa?

- Do you have trouble untangling your own emotions and opinions from those around you?

- Do you tend to avoid or dislike violent or negative broadcasts, movies or stories?

- Do you tend to have difficulty making decisions or do you sometimes suffer with mental confusion?

- Do you feel that you regularly ride an emotional rollercoaster?

- Do you notice that you often feel vague or light-headed?

- Have you often been told that you are 'too sensitive' or 'over emotional'?

- Are you attracted to spiritual subjects such as crystals, energy healing or Angels?

If you answered 'yes' to most of these questions you are a sensitive and would benefit from some help with managing and understanding your sensitivity. If you answered 'yes' to about half of these then you are probably experiencing an opening of your intuition and sensitivity; the exercises in this book will help you to do this painlessly and relatively quickly. Even if you answered 'yes' to only a few of the questions, this book will help you to learn to develop your own sensitivity, intuition or healing ability.

The techniques here are ideal for everyone who is interested in becoming a more connected, sensitive and aware individual, or assist you to understand other people who experience sensitivity.

The above questions are all situations and reactions that sensitive people often struggle with. As a sensitive being, you can wonder what you are doing here on this planet where people can seem to behave in such insensitive and harsh ways. Busy places like public transport or a shopping centre are challenging and emotionally draining experiences; talking to a depressed friend can be exhausting.

Sometimes emotions and physical feelings can run through your body that seemingly come from nowhere. Your mind and emotions can feel like a tangled ball of wool. You dream of complete peace and solitude, and perhaps contemplate moving to a remote mountain cabin with only a cat for company! Animals and nature offer a welcome sanctuary in an apparently disturbed world.

As a spiritual and sensitive being, you can feel so elated and connected in one moment yet disconnected and heavy the next. This happens because your energetic and physical systems become clogged with negative energy from outside yourself. Negative energy has the effect of bringing you down, like a cloud passing in front the sun it affects your self-esteem and wellbeing. As you absorb this energy, your mind and intuition become fuzzy and doubts begin to creep in. You waiver between being tuned in to your sensitive higher self that always knows the truth that all is well and you are safe, to listening to your ego fears which look for negativity and tell you that you are unsafe.

Sensitive people can feel like misfits, not only because of the way they respond to foods, energy and the world around them but also because of their interests. You may be strongly attracted to subjects that the people around you find strange and unimportant, such as spirituality, new age healing, art, music, environmental subjects, animal welfare, and social justice. These subjects can represent a passionate drive for a sensitive: by pursuing them, they find relief from their difficulties. Others may mock or question your interests whilst you cannot explain why you love and need them so much, they may not make sense on a practical level.

You may feel repelled by things that friends and family enjoy such as action or horror movies, loud music, city shopping, and news publications and so on. In the face of controversy, you might live a kind of double life or even deny your attraction to what you want in order to go with the crowd.

If your sensitivity manifests physically, you can have the challenge of dealing with allergies and intolerances, unexplained illnesses, pain and other bodily reactions. These responses can be to additives in food and beverages, stimulants such as caffeine, alcohol, nicotine, pollutants in the environment, and chemicals in cleaning products and toiletries, a toxic emotional situation, or even a certain room or building. These reactions can strongly affect a sensitive person's health and even become debilitating. These responses are your sensitivity giving you a clear message and should be investigated rather than ignored.

The Sensitive guidance system

Being sensitive actually means that you are fitted with an inbuilt receiver and guidance system; a sixth sense, which receives information from around and within you. It tells you information, including what is good and what is not good for you. Obviously, discomfort alerts you to what does not personally enhance your experience and positive feelings guide you towards what will!

Of course every human has this inbuilt guidance system but if you are sensitive it is turned up extra loud so that you cannot and should not ignore it. Your energetic being (comprising your body, emotions and auric field) absorbs information like a sponge and your internal guidance system interprets it and 'talks' to you through your thoughts, emotions, and physical body. As you become more adept at 'listening', you may then detect other signals such as clairvoyant visions, and auditory psychic messages.

All of this receiving and absorbing of energy has a very powerful effect, especially if you do not know how to manage and interpret it. Most sensitives do not understand what is happening to them, only that they often feel very uncomfortable and unbalanced. Over time your aura, mind, emotions and body can become congested with energy from within and outside yourself. This can manifest as feelings of being overwhelmed, fatigue or even pain.

Ordinary tasks then become difficult and daunting. It is in these circumstances that you may feel the urge to withdraw. This is your intuition's way of telling you that you must not absorb any more energy and you need to clear yourself. In essence, you are 'full up'. If withdrawal and clearing is not possible or you leave it too long then you can become depressed, angry or may turn to addictive or compulsive behaviours to cope.

You may have learned to fight your natural urges and feelings to tolerate unpleasant circumstances because at some stage you have told yourself that your own opinions and feelings are unimportant. This is because you do not trust your own inner guidance system and you have learned to override and deny your sensitive feelings. If this is the case you may stay too long in negative situations, eat foods that are toxic to your body or even act in ways that are against your deeper truth and integrity. These behaviours can create enormous internal confusion and pain. In these situations, you may become depressed, ill and feel that you are completely off track with your life. This is when the universe will try to get your attention with a painful situation designed to wake you up and bring you to awareness of the level of imbalance in your life. When you do not listen to the clear and intelligent guidance system that speaks through your sensitivity, you are effectively blinding your intuition. This leads to confusion and you may find that you over rely on other sources for decision-making and advice. This can result in an over dependency in unhealthy relationships (co-dependence), indecision, procrastination or an over reliance on psychics, counsellors and other professionals. Many try to further numb out the pain with addictive behaviours.

Each step that is taken away from your inner truth takes you further away from your life path and will create more pain and confusion. The consequence of ignoring the guidance and numbing your sensitivity creates other negative side effects and the messages become stronger in order to grab your attention.

The happy news is that no-one can switch off his or her internal guidance. It keeps on sending messages in an effort to keep you healthy, happy, energised and peacefully aligned with the true you. In a sense it is a good friend, a guide; it is actually the true you! It never gives up!

Many energy sensitive people curse their sensitivity and feel that they need to 'toughen up' as friends and relatives tease or criticise them for their reactions. The truth is all that you really need is to listen to this guidance and follow it, become even more sensitive and encourage others to do the same.

It is impossible to desensitise completely, and doing so only creates more problems. Trying to switch off this valuable tool results in pain as your inner self struggles to get your attention!

The only successful way forwards is to accept and embrace your sensitive internal guidance system and learn to manage your energy field and clear away the effects of negativity and other people's energy on yours.

Once you have learnt how to manage your energy, you will:

- Know how to protect and discern your feelings and thoughts from those around you.

- Know how to protect your energy field from outside influence.

- Easily listen to what your feelings and thoughts are telling you and trust their guidance.

- Be able to make simple decisions that will guide you towards your highest good in every way.

- Be able to clear yourself regularly so that you can remain grounded and centred.

- Feel stronger, healthier and more confident.

- Be walking your true path.

Once harnessed, your sensitivity will bless you in so many ways.

Your wonderful internal guidance system will steer you unerringly towards happiness and fulfilment.

The blessings of honouring your sensitivity:

- You will trust yourself.

- You will have the confidence and guidance to make good decisions.

- You will understand and love yourself more.

- You will have stronger boundaries.

- You will know your life purpose.

- You will be clear minded.

- Your intuition and psychic ability will open up.

- You will be able to connect to your angels and guides if you want to.

- You will learn about your energy and how to use it to heal.

- Your connection with nature, animals and children will increase.

- Your health and vitality will improve.

- Your relationships will improve.

- You will become stronger and self reliant.

- You will begin to attract more of what you want with the laws of attraction.

- You will become aware of the gift of being sensitive and learn to manage it so that it becomes a reliable guidance tool.

With this knowledge, your world will reveal itself as the peaceful, harmonious and gentle place it really is, where you can manifest your desires and needs easily and life will flow.

The psychic connection

Your sensitive receptivity can be developed to include psychic and healing ability. Many sensitives are able to connect and tune into spiritual realms and beings such as angels and deceased loved ones. This ability is called clairsentience and it means to feel clearly. However, all intuition can be developed to become clearer and skills learned to ensure that the clairsentient is adequately protected.

All forms of psychic ability are based on sensing and trusting messages that come through various channels or senses. A clairvoyant receives visual messages, in their minds eye or with their physical eyes, a clairaudient receives audio messages, and a claircognisant receives messages as thoughts and knowledge.

Clairsentients receive physical and emotional feelings from the world around them. Clairsentients must be highly sensitive to receive messages of this type. Sensitivity is a powerful gift and like all gifts can be nurtured and developed.

Most psychics have at least one strong channel and are able to develop the others to varying degrees with practice and self-knowledge and by increasing their sensitivity.

Even if you do not feel that you are psychic, you are certainly able to develop your sensitivity to receive psychic messages if you want to. You are already using your intuition on some level, especially if you are able to feel other people's emotions. Sensitivity is really intuition talking to you through your thoughts, feelings, emotions, and physical body.

Clairsentience is also known as empathy. To be empathic means to be able to feel what another person is feeling, literally. This can include physical and emotional feelings. Empathic people are often natural healers as they are loving and compassionate with an instinctive desire to help people, animals and the planet. The ability to sense physical and emotional needs is often combined with a knowledge (claircognisance) of how to heal the area of need or at least an interest in healing modalities such as crystals, Reiki, massage, or more traditional forms like nursing, counselling or nutrition.

The techniques described in the following chapters will help you to gain awareness of your self; they can increase your intuition so that you can better manage your own life. You will also develop a connection to the spiritual healing and energetic realm and learn how to create positive experiences with the Law of Attraction.

Sensitive children

This knowledge about energy and healing is relevant to all sensitive people including children and their parents and carers, if you work in a career caring for others, teaching, or healing you will be able to use some of the knowledge and techniques to heighten your own intuition and to understand your clients or students.

Many children are extremely sensitive to energy, emotions, foods, and their environments. These children have been called Indigo and Crystal children and are described as new generations. They are so sensitive that they are unable to override their feelings and instead have extreme reactions that are very problematic to their wellbeing and block their ability to enjoy their lives.

Society generally does not understand these children and why they behave as they do. They are often misdiagnosed or unwittingly mistreated. They need awareness, understanding and training in how to manage and work with this sensitivity. Their parents and carers need to understand so that they can make the best choices and bring harmony back to their families.

These children can feel so much and are so affected by energy or toxins in their foods, medicines and environments that they can become crippled emotionally, physically and mentally.

From an outsider's perspective, they may appear to be being difficult, having tantrums, withdrawing, failing at school, acting out, suffering with depression, a disease or disorder or just plain weird. They are in fact desperately crying out for help as their pure sensitive bodies are impacted by a fury of energy that they cannot determine or control.

Many reactions can be traced to a sensitivity issue. For instance a child who is having trouble sleeping may be sensitive to the energy and emotions of the family or school friends. Electronic devices, spirit beings or the decor in their bedrooms may disturb them.

Food additives, cleaning products or even sounds, can disrupt their delicate systems. There are many things that can influence the human energy field. Understanding and managing sensitivity in children can make a profound difference to their behaviour, self-esteem and later life choices. If a child is taught early on that his or her intuitive responses are real and important and to listen to (not override) his or her internal guidance system, it will keep them safer, healthier and self reliant.

In my experience, when a sensitive child discovers the truth about their sensitivity and learns some simple techniques to manage their energy they immediately feel better. They can gain more focus, optimism and direction and can feel good about themselves knowing that they are not 'weird' or broken. They can learn to trust their feelings and how to separate theirs from others which empowers them and frees up their emotional energy.

Wanting to go home

A sensitive person can believe that they do not fit in this world and somehow is not supposed to be here. This can lead to depression and even suicidal thoughts[1].

Often very sensitive people are psychic. They know themselves to be spiritual beings in a physical body and have memories of how life was on 'the other side' or at 'home' before they incarnated as a physical being. In this instance, 'home' is the place we existed before this physical life and return to upon death: A spiritual place of loving gentle energy where harshness and pain are not present. These memories combined with the shock of some harsh event can result in depression and trigger a deep yearning to 'go home' to this loving Utopia.

People experiencing these kinds of thoughts, memories and feelings may or may not be conscious of them but will act them out in a number of ways. One coping mechanism is to spend a lot of time 'floating' in between worlds. To an outsider they seem to be unfocussed, switched off or in a daydream. In truth, they have become ungrounded and are losing connection with their physical body in an attempt to reach the spiritual realms or disassociate from what they feel is harsh energy in their life. This creates a scattered kind of energy, as they are neither here nor there! Alternatively they may withdraw from others and spend lots of time alone. A healthy response is to create a sacred space to recharge and renew the energy, and to pursue activities that affirm your beautiful sensitive nature. This might be spending time in nature, listening to music, creativity, meditation, and play with animals or children.

1 Please note: If you are experiencing suicidal thoughts then please seek support and professional help and similarly if you know someone who is depressed or suicidal then encourage them to do the same. Depression should be taken seriously no matter what the cause.

Everyone has a right to gentle and loving life circumstances but it is easy to feel a sense of hopelessness and loss of control when you are barraged with harshness and surrounded with things that do not validate you. This kind of homesickness is often healed once your feelings and memories are acknowledged and validated, perhaps by like-minded friends or a healer.

It is important to recognise you chose to be here on earth at this particular time for a particular reason and that you are not alone. It is also important to learn to ground your energy and be in the physical realm whilst nurturing your sensitivity and developing psychically for an effective connection to 'home'.

This knowledge and confirmation certainly helped me and has helped others to have the strength and inspiration to move through these feelings and focus on the present moment and the joy of living this wonderful life!

A wonderful antidote is to connect to other sensitive people so that you do not feel so alone. To meet like minds, join meditation groups, art classes, spiritual churches, healing courses or seek spiritual groups on line. Trust your intuition to ensure that they are supportive and high in integrity.

The purpose of sensitivity

This is an important time on planet earth; sensitivity or perhaps 'desensitisation' are issues at the core of many social, environmental and personal challenges. Allergies and intolerances, disorders, disease and mental illness abound as bodies and minds show signs of stress, toxicity and overload. Our beautiful planet has suffered, as we, her guardians, pollute and raid her resources without understanding the consequences for her sensitive body and our existence. So many worldly and social issues are calling out for attention, with the environment in particular showing signs of discord. How long can we switch off to these signs and how loud do they have to get before everyone takes notice? We must recognise and remember that we are a part of an interconnected whole system and that we need our sensitivity to truly live in harmony with each other and the planet.

Everybody has the ability to use feelings to guide them. Humankind now has no choice.

Sensitivity is a valuable and accurate tool, we all have emotions and feelings that speak to us on every subject and whether you are sensitive or not you can use the techniques and information within these pages to develop this tool and translate your intuitive guidance.

It is time to tune into what our hearts and souls are telling us in each moment so we can heal each other, the earth and ourselves.

Chapter 2

Angels

Angels are spiritual beings of pure love and light, and for this reason I have included them in this book. When you call upon angels they can help you to dissolve the effects of negative energy in your life and help you to remain sensitive but protected.

They are loving guardians and guides who love to work in service to and in cooperation with, humanity. I have witnessed many powerful healings take place in the lives of sensitive people through working with angels.

Angels are our co-creators, they never take over our lives but seek to empower us to improve and heal our own situations. They will answer our prayers for assistance by arranging synchronicities, creating opportunities and offering guidance, of course it is up to us to recognise and follow the guidance, in this way we are empowered, and in control of our own life direction.

Everyone has guardian angels and can call upon their assistance. There are no special rules, religious affiliation or skills needed in order to pray for help. Angels will respond to your requests immediately, whether you can sense them or not. All that is needed is an open mind and little faith, your faith will increase as you recognise that your prayers are being answered, though perhaps not in the way you imagined!

Although organised religions describe angels in their writings, angels are non-denominational. Divine beings are mentioned throughout history in many spiritual manuscripts as messengers, protectors and guides, sometimes with wings and light surrounding them.

The word angel means 'messenger of God'. Divine angels are so pure and loving because they are from the source that many people identify as God or the universe. It does not matter what beliefs you hold about angels or God, spiritual help is available to everyone. Angelic loving energy is very high in vibration; just by calling upon angels, you improve your life as they bring this love into everything you do.

Healing with angels

Healing is heightened and enhanced when angels are invited to the process. Almost all of the techniques described in this book are angel psychic healing visualisations that work in a powerful way. You do not have to have a strong belief in angels or be great at visualisation in order for these methods to succeed. The important ingredients are a positive intention and an open mind.

When you invite angels and archangels to a healing session, the highest and purest vibrations of love are palpable even if you are not able to fully see and hear them. This is because angels are divine beings of love. The atmosphere of pure love that they bring is the perfect condition for healing to take place. Invoking angels brings complete protection to everyone present and intensifies the effects of the healing.

The angels work through the healer and guide their actions and words, they also work on the client on many levels enabling a release of lower energies and constantly clearing the room and both parties, so that the energy remains loving and light.

You have two or more beautiful loving guardian angels standing beside you right now. These loving compassionate guides stay with you throughout your human life, wrapping you in a loving protective light and watching over you, guiding your decisions.

Your guardian angels know all about you but they are not judgmental or critical. As beings of divine love, they do not experience the human ego feelings such as judgement, anger or fear. They always see you in your highest light and love you unconditionally because they have no other perspective.

The absence of ego allows healing to occur; only our lower ego self believes in the illusion of illness or pain. The angels hold the truth of perfect healing like a bright torch of light over you so that you can experience this truth in the form of healing. They lend us these conditions temporarily so that we can experience the release of lower vibrations.

They make perfect guides and confidantes as they know you so well and they can see the bigger picture of your life such as your life purpose and your soul's needs and hearts passions.

You can act as an earth angel by holding the vision that all things negative are actually an illusion and that underneath there only exists the truth: love. This is a very powerful tool in healing any form of discord, if you can affirm 'all is well in truth' and pray for angelic assistance, in the face of any seemingly negative or bad situation you will help to bring about this truth.

It is actually the human ego focus on 'what is wrong' that adds energy to negative events. With a focus on love without ego judgement you can transform your own life and bring healing to others. Ask your angels to help you quiet your ego voice and only see the love in everything and everyone. Soon you will discover that this becomes the truth for you.

Archangels

Archangels are like the management team of the angelic realm. They are large and powerful divine beings that can be invoked and prayed to just as your guardian angels. Your prayers will always be answered and an Archangel will immediately assist you in healing your life situation.

The Archangels have individual areas of speciality such as healing, harmony, helping pets, clearing away negativity, teaching spiritual laws, healing grief and other forms of emotional healing.

Archangels are multi-dimensional and can be with many people at the same time, so when you call upon them trust that they will be with you! It does not matter whether you can see or sense their presence — they will be there!

They always have strong, positive and healing guidance for each situation. I invoke them to assist with my healing, teaching and guidance sessions and send them to be with people in need with fast and wonderful results.

The two Archangels that I regularly call upon to assist with healing sensitivity and energy are the Archangel Michael and the Archangel Raphael.

Archangel Michael has a warm strong and direct energy.

I would describe him as a powerful warrior without the aggression. This highly powerful and protective angel carries a sword of light, which he uses to clear away lower energies. He can appear as a dark purple and royal blue light; these are the colours of his aura.

You can borrow these colours to protect and heighten your own energy field. Ask him to help you to clear negativity from your life and pray to him to protect you when you feel vulnerable. He will be there without delay!

Archangel Raphael works wonderfully in concert with Michael. As the sweet natured leader of the healing angels, Raphael will guide you in your healing process and send healing light to assist in the rapid recovery from all physical and emotional pain and disease. Call upon Raphael if you or a family member is unwell.

It is particularly useful to ask him to join you at medical or healing appointments. Many healers have the loving energy of Archangel Raphael with them, who appears as a bright clean green tint in the aura. Visualise this soothing light surrounding anyone who is in need of healing; it will dissolve pain and disease. Archangel Raphael reminds me to mention that he is very willing to heal your pets.

You can invoke other Archangels depending on the issue. Sometimes you will attract the guidance of a certain archangel through your life purpose or prayers. For example, a nurse could have Archangel Raphael with her to assist in her healing work, or a young girl who feels vulnerable might have attracted Archangel Michael to her side. If you do not know which Archangel to invoke then just ask for the area of need such as the 'healing angels', the 'car repair angels' or the 'meditation angels', for example.

All angels are pure love and light you need not fear invoking the wrong sort of angel. There is no such thing! The precise reason that I choose to work with angels because their love forms a protective barrier whereby no lower vibrating energies can enter! White light, which is traditionally used in protection, is actually divine angel energy. Surround yourself or your room or home with this light and you will have no fear of a lower energy invading.

Fear is the lowest vibrating energy and love is the highest. When you work with love, fear simply cannot exist as it is vibrating at a much lower rate. This is why angel energy is so effective in clearing away lower vibrating human emotions and their effects.

Sensitive people can have very effective results from working with angels and archangels because they provide protection and clear away the fear based energies that affect empathic people so much. Sensitivity is a perfect tool to tune into the divine angelic energy.

Angel invocation

You do not need special words or skills to invoke angels, just politely ask their help and outline the details of the situation that you would like help with. It is not necessary to tell them how you want them to help you as this is up to divine will. Your angels will find the best, quickest and happiest solution for all concerned. You can invoke angels on the behalf of others or yourself. It is especially powerful to state your specific intentions in the invocation.

Example angel invocations

I now ask for the presence of Archangel Michael, Archangel Michael. I now intend to clear my home and body of negativity. Please come to my side and help me to clear this area of any lower energy, please surround my home with your protective light. I ask for your guidance in my life in staying safe and protected, and I promise to be open to your messages. Thank you for protecting my home and me. Amen.

I now ask for the presence of Archangel Raphael and the healing angels. Angels I now intend to send healing to my friend (name), Please help me to send this energy, go to her side, guide her to the best practitioners if necessary, completely heal her of all illusions of pain and illness, help us all to have faith. Thank you for healing my friend, amen.

I now ask for the presence of my Guardian Angels and the career angels. Angels I intend to find my life purpose, please help me with guidance, and lead me to the knowledge, people and information that I need to find and work on my life purpose. Please increase my trust and faith. Thank you for helping me amen.

I now ask for the presence of the relationship Angels, Angels I intend to heal the conflict in my love relationship. Help me to bring peace and love into this relationship. Give us both guidance and healing. Thank you for healing this relationship amen.

An invocation prayer ensures the presence of the Angels and clearly states your intentions. You are effectively adding power to your prayers.

How to tell that angels are around

The angels will let you know that they are around you in subtle ways. As a sensitive, you will easily notice these signs through your feelings. Angels are pure love and light so their energy is easy to detect, however it is easier to connect with them when your energy is clean and cleared of clutter. When there is a lot of heavy energy around it is harder to detect their higher vibrations. You can open your energy through regular meditation and practicing the cleansing, shielding and grounding methods in chapter 5. When you sense an angel you will likely find it an emotional experience as they transmit unconditional love to you, you may also feel warmth or tingling on your body. Clairvoyants see bright light, angel wings or even a whole angel in their minds eye or in front of them if they are highly developed. Clairaudients hear the angel's voice.

Signs that angels are talking to you

It does not matter whether your psychic senses are tuned in or not, when you are open and willing to connect to your angels, they will contact you through signs in the physical world. Here are some examples of signs that the angels are talking to you:

- Finding white feathers;

- Noticing a twinkle of white light out of the corner of your eye;

- Seeing references to angels everywhere you go;

- Seeing a glowing orb of coloured light;

- Synchronicities in answer to your prayers;

- Flickering light bulbs;

- An unexplained light orb in photographs;

- Angel shaped cloud formations;

- Hearing a repetitive song on the radio that has a message or meaning to you.

Angels have unlimited ways of talking to you but each sign is accompanied with an inner knowing, warmth or goose bumps that tell you that they are genuine. Your body always responds to the truth. I once asked for a sign at a deserted beach and moments later found a perfect sand angel imprint in the dunes. There were no footprints or other indication that anyone else had been there. It was a windy day; the sand angel was only about two foot tall!

Things to remember about angels:

- Angels are governed by the Law of Freewill and need to be asked to intervene; this is one reason why prayer is so powerful!

- Angels want to help you, so release any guilt you may have about asking for help!

- Angels embody the highest vibrations of pure light and love.

- Angels have no judgement or anger; they come entirely from universal love.

- Angels will never ask you to do something detrimental to yourself or another.

- Angels will not take control of your life but will give you guidance or assistance that empowers you!

- You do not have to have certain beliefs, practices or special skills to invoke angels.

- Ask for signs that your angels are around you.

- Angels love you unconditionally, never leave you and are with you right now!

Angels and the Law of Attraction

Angels can help you to reach your goals and attract your desires through the Law of Attraction. The universal Law of Attraction is completely unbiased and unwavering: whatever you think about and focus your energies upon you will receive, whether it is good or bad; you will always receive the results of these thoughts without fail. Until you master your thoughts and energies this can be a haphazard experience whereby you attract lots of what you do not want, some of what you do want and lots of unforseen things by default!

The angels, however, are compassionate and powerful masters of manifestation and they have the advantage of an overview of your life, thoughts, beliefs and energy. Their loving vibrations are exactly the energies required to dissolve negativity and attract more of what you want!

All too often, our lower ego fears get in the way of our manifestations, such as negative beliefs about our lack of worth or fears that we may not receive what we are asking for.

You can ask your angels to help you to overcome these tendencies. In answer to such prayers, they might increase your vibration so that you attract experiences that are more loving, they will help you to release negative thought patterns, or perhaps filter your thoughts and ultimately assist you in manifesting your goals in a gentle way. They will help you to know what you want and they will help you to know how to get it, they will even arrange synchronicities, support and guidance to help you along the way! In this way, you approach your manifesting and attracting with a powerful and loving coach that can guide you gently through the process.

How Angel Healing works

You can easily invoke angels for yourself or on behalf of someone else. The energy is just as powerful. However all healing involves a willingness to heal on behalf of the recipient. Healing is a personal matter of choice or freewill made at a soul or a physical level. This means that at some level you have made a choice to experience every life condition that you encounter, even the painful ones!

This is not to say that you need to continue to suffer or that you cannot make a better choice. It may be that you have chosen unconsciously because of a mistaken belief or thought, you may have chosen by default because of fearful thoughts. You may not be consciously aware where the thought or belief has come from or even that you have a choice!

Fear energy, such as guilt, resentment, lack of forgiveness or anger, is the root cause of all pain and disease of any kind. Pain can include emotional pain, financial issues, relationship stress and any condition that feels unpleasant. This fear energy becomes solidified in the aura and eventually the body as pain or illness. It also manifests outside reflected in the way people seem to treat you or in your financial situation. The energy can become thicker and heavier as it attracts similar thought forms and energies.

This energy and its root cause cannot be released without your willingness or permission.

Usually a person suffering pain is very willing to release the source of their pain especially when they become aware of the negative effects that the fear energy is having. They often need reminding that they can let go of the negative emotion attached to a situation and replace it with a more positive energy such as love, peace or abundance. The angels help with this as they communicate love and peace.

You have an inner being – the true higher self who is pure divine love. This inner being always wants the most loving healed outcome. Your ego self has forgotten the true state of love and lives in fear believing the illusions of pain and illness and negativity.

The very presence of loving divine angels allows the higher self to give permission for the whole person to release the fear energy. There only has to be the tiniest bit of willingness for this healing to take place. The ego has no power in the presence of pure love and truth.

There are many reasons why another person may not be willing to accept healing, and it is important to respect their freewill.

Sometimes it is simply their time to pass into spirit and they have already decided when and how this will happen. Sometimes an individual may not be ready to release the fear or may believe that the fear protects them in some way. Some are attached to fear or illness because they believe it gives their life some meaning. On occasion, a being has made a soul contract before incarnation to go through a personal challenge such as illness or trauma, even perhaps with other people who are a part of the seeming drama. It is equally important to understand that it is not necessary to experience pain or limitation for spiritual growth. The angels wish you to know that you need not suffer in any way and that karma does not require you to pay for past mistakes. Karma is a spiritual law of cause and effect not reward and punishment. Karma simply allows you to release the cause of negative effects!

No matter what the individual belief system any angel healing that you send to someone can never harm or 'foil' freewill and choice. In fact the clearing of fear and the addition of loving energy will always help the transition or process of each individual journey; the healing will 'hang' in the aura until the recipient is ready to accept it.

Disease or pain occurs when you believe a fear scenario presented by your or another person's ego. Illusions such as victim hood, illness, abuse and death, lead you to believe that you are in danger and helpless. In truth, you are timeless, whole, and powerful and it is impossible to lose anything or be less than or better than anyone! This may seem untrue because the illusion seems so real but as soon as you choose to look for the higher truth, healing can begin to occur.

When love is present via the angels it allows for all your illusionary fearful thoughts to be released and exchanged for more love.
An angel healing will have a ripple effect in your life. Your new receptive state of wellbeing and love can attract abundance, health, love, intuition and a stronger connection to your angels and God. The truth of wholeness is restored and with that comes solid manifestations in the form of abundance, love, happiness and fulfilment.

Case study: Geraldine

Here is an example of how introducing angels to your life with some energy management techniques can change everything for the better:

Geraldine, a sensitive light worker, was suffering from a myriad of negative feelings and just not feeling like her old self. She was experiencing irritation, anger, tiredness and was having relationship problems. Geraldine was smoking and drinking to cope. She was depressed and 'foggy' with no clear direction. She disliked her work as retail assistant in a busy centre although she loved people.

We began with clearing her energy and connecting with her angels for insight to her issues. They showed us that she was absorbing a lot of negative energy from her customers at the shopping centre and was struggling with her partner's anger issues. Geraldine began clearing her energy and grounding and shielding regularly and connecting to her angels for guidance. A few months later she was stronger happier and had clear direction. She quit her work, cleared up her relationship and moved interstate to study for her dream job; everything fell into place for her.

It is so powerful to invite angels into your world. Talk to them, pray to them, ask for their help and keep pictures of them around you. Their divine presence reminds you who you really are: a powerful peaceful being of love, and lifts your vibration to attract more loving situations and people towards you.

As you give them permission to intervene, angels can help to heal all aspects of your life and soon you will wonder what you ever did without them!

For those that seem to be a victim of their feelings and live in deep emotional or physical pain, then my wish is that this information and these healing techniques will set you free.

Angels in action

Anne was feeling lost, vague and depressed with crying bouts that seemed to have no origin. She is very sensitive and in tune with her angels but was unable to detect where this heavy energy was coming from.

During the Angel Psychic Healing session, the angels showed me that Anne had retained some negative energy from grief that she had experienced a number of years ago. They psychically showed me a book and ornate pen, when I asked Anne she remembered that she had a journal and special pen in her home that she had used to express her fear when her partner had passed away. Anne then psychically released the book and pen to the angels, they then cleared and shielded her energy. She was given instructions to burn the book when she went home. Anne's positive mood and energy immediately returned after the session.

Case study: Tanya

Tanya came to me for a massage on her tight neck. She divulged that she was suffering stress as a result of nightmares, terrors and extreme anxiety and fear. This fear stemmed from having been told the details of a movie about a girl who was supposedly 'possessed' by a ghost. Since hearing about this Tanya feared that the same could happen to her. Her extreme sensitivity had absorbed the fear from this movie via another person and she was unable to detach from it. In our sessions we cleared away the fear energy and associated ties. I introduced Tanya to Archangel Michael and gave her advice to protect, clear and ground her energies. With healing sessions and through learning about sensitivity and angels, Tanya was finally able to overcome her fear. She has incorporated these practices into her life and has since joyfully discovered her life purpose with children, spiritual work and healed many other challenges in her life!

Chapter 3

What is energy?

Energy is all around us, constantly flowing; it makes up everything we know. Science has shown that even the most solid items of matter are actually vibrating particles. Even those things that cannot be seen have energy vibrations such as thoughts, emotions and sounds.

Humans are energetic beings. Physical flesh and bone is a dense form of energy. Our life force energy, which is a higher vibrating energy, invisible to our usual physical vision flows through our bodies through chakras (energy centres) via energetic veins called meridian lines. We are surrounded by an energetic etheric field known as the aura that reaches out as an extension of our physical and energetic form.

This etheric energy field contains information about your whole being. Its size, shape, colours and behaviour are determined by your thoughts, beliefs, feelings, physical emotional and mental health, relationships, history and actions. Some of the information contained in your aura is unconscious, in other words, you are unaware of it, yet your energy field transmits this information. Your aura is your signature, and it is the part of you that everyone meets first.

Sensitive people can read auras through their own senses and will react to whatever they find there, often unintentionally.

You are entirely an energetic being and your whole being is connected. You cannot have an effect to one part of the energetic or physical body without the other.

Traditional Western teaching and medicine has historically overlooked the energetic side of human nature and focuses mainly on the physical. This is certainly changing and many energy healing modalities are now widely available,.

Some examples are; Reiki, Qi Gong, Applied Kinesiology, colour therapy, crystal healing, bush flower essences and acupuncture, to name just a few. All of these therapies work on an energetic level to help correct imbalances and disease.

Intuitive and spiritually aligned individuals recognise energy and auras as real and important to our overall wellbeing. Energy is as obvious as a smell or taste to those who are sensitive to it.

Through developing intuitive senses like clairvoyance and clairsentience, everyone can begin to see, feel and sense differences in energy and interpret its meanings. Most people are aware of energy on some level. We can intuitively tell when someone's energy is low and respond to people with high or inspiring energy. Most people will talk about the energy of a particular room or location especially if it is strongly negative or positive.

Everyone and everything including animals and plants have a distinctive energy signature. It is invisible to most but clearly sensed. Aura photography can take a picture of the energetic field of plants and people with a special type of sensitive electronic camera. These photographs show an energetic field around living organisms. It was found that the energy field changed in strength and colours depending on health and emotional states.

The energy of emotions

Your energy field is influenced by all of your thoughts and emotions. As a conscious being everything begins with thought. Thoughts and emotions have vibrations. An angry thought will

create an angry feeling, the longer you think the angry thoughts the stronger the feeling and the accompanying vibration becomes. Joy has a very different higher vibration that affects your body in a different way. It does not matter whether you are thinking about the past or the present; the negative or positive thought will create emotional energy right now and effect your present vibration. Experiments have shown that the body cannot tell whether an event is actually happening or is being remembered or visualised — the physiological responses are the same!

When a thought and accompanying emotional vibration is held for long enough it begins to manifest into form into your life. This is the Law of Attraction. Hence, angry persons tend to attract more situations to be angry about. As a lower vibrating energy, negativity within your thoughts and energy will also serve to block and repel any positive situations that you wish to attract.

You already know that love and fear feel completely different within your body and emanating from another person. Tibetan monks radiate joy and compassion and generally, people tend to avoid angry or miserable people.

Emotions feel so different because they vibrate differently. The closer the feeling is to love then the higher and lighter the vibration. Higher and lighter vibrations are healing and energising. They sweep away the low energies. Lower emotions come from fear and are heavy and dark. They tend to obstruct your energetic system often manifesting into physical and emotional blockages.

For instance, a person holding onto long-term anger or fear may manifest an illness, depression or fatigue as the heavy energy coagulates in the system.

Energy healing methods work by clearing away the lower energies using the highest vibration of all: Love.

Lower forms of energy all originate from fear, the opposite of love. Fear is the belief in the absence of love. Love and wellbeing are always available and present. As a low vibrational blockage, fear acts like a cloud blocking the sun.

In our material reality, particularly when we vibrate with low energy, fear can seem real and blocks us from feeling the love that is always there. You cannot feel love so you believe it is gone. However even on a cloudy day you never believe that the sun has completely disappeared!

The health and behaviour of your auric field, begins with the energy of your own thoughts and emotions and determines whether you attract or repel positive experiences such as good health, happy relationships, abundance and success.

You can see why it is so important to focus on loving thoughts and clear away negativity and other unwanted energy that you may have collected or absorbed.

How emotional energy effects a Sensitive

As a sensitive person, you can feel and may even absorb negative emotions into your body and auric field that are transmitted from other people. If you are highly receptive, you can even feel energy from locations and items that hold the emotional energetic imprint of the people and actions that took place there.

These feelings can then affect your whole energy system and bring down your vibration, attracting more fear-based thoughts towards you if they are not released regularly. This is one of the many reasons why a sensitive can feel drained, heavy or emotional.

Entrainment

You already know that energy can be absorbed and passed from one place to another, which is one reason why, as a sensitive, you can have a difficult time with other people's negative emotions. However, there is another way in which outside energy can affect you; Entrainment.

Entrainment occurs when your personal energy field aligns itself with another energy vibration and begins to vibrate at the same level. An example of entrainment occurs when women living or working together begin to menstruate at the same time as their cycles synchronise. Mechanical clocks in the same vicinity often adjust themselves over time to match one another.

Entrainment means that your vibration synchronises with the strongest vibration around you. Entrainment can be the cause for feeling drained and low in energy after spending time in negative environments. You can literally align with negativity and begin to feel low. It is important to be aware of entrainment especially if you are working to heal negative thoughts. If you have a past pattern of negativity, it is easy to 'drop' to the lower levels of negative thinking when introduced to it by outside influences because the vibration is familiar to you. When you become aware of this it is important to learn to energetically clear and protect yourself and perhaps even avoid negative situations until you become stronger in your positive vibration.

Every situation is a potential life lesson and if you do find that you have entrained to a lower vibration then let go of guilt or judgement (low vibrating emotions), clear yourself and use positive affirmations, music, nature and other positive methods to uplift your vibration again. The ideal scenario is to entrain others to your higher vibration, which is effectively, what happens during a healing, the healer holds a positive vibration of love and healing and helps bring the client into alignment with it.

Remember that you are never a helpless victim of others even when it comes to entrainment; you always have a choice in how you respond once you are aware of how your energy behaves.

Energy to fuel your life

Many people complain that they are low on energy. A lack of vitality can have many causes for instance an unhealthy diet, lack of sleep, too much stress, depression or a sedentary life style. It is crucially important to take responsibility for your body, mind and emotions by taking good care of your physical self.

Emotional and spiritual energy also have an impact on your vitality within your body and your energy field. Depending on its vibration and source, emotional energy can drive and nourish you in the same way that organic and fresh food gives your body fuel. Nature is a source of this energy, an inspiring or spiritual movie, seminar, music or book can energise you emotionally with passion or excitement – which then gives more power to your physical body. A sad or traumatic event can have the opposite effect so that no matter how many kilojoules you eat, you can still feel flat if you focus on the sadness. All energy affects your moods, wellbeing and physical health.

You are given enough life force energy to fulfil all of your needs through out your whole life on earth. As long as you are eating healthily, exercising and getting enough sleep, a lack of energy probably means that you are somehow connecting to or dwelling in lower vibration emotions creating a block or imbalance in your energy field. This fatigue can lead to a search for replenishment from outside sources.

Our life force energy comes from an infinite source; some call this source God, the Great Spirit, the Universe or the Divine. This same source creates enough air to breath and causes nature to flourish. We are all constantly connected to this supply of pure love and therefore given the means to recharge and remain permanently energised at all times.

Most people do not understand this source of energy or their connection to it and cut themselves off with negative, fearful behaviours and thoughts. These lower vibrations are the real cause of the perceived lack of energy. When feeling low in energy most people only understand that they want to feel better so they consciously or unconsciously seek outside supplies in order to raise their vibration and replenish. These false energy sources only provide a short-lived boost. This search for outer energy is the reason behind much addictive and self-destructive behaviour.

When you consciously reconnect to the true Source you automatically balance yourself. This will simultaneously heal feelings of insecurity or lack.

Reconnection visualisation

Imagine yourself as a being of pure energy and light, see yourself completely surrounded and protected by your auric field. There is one thick long tube of light emanating from your aura just above the top of your head and travelling up to the true Source. You are constantly energised by light through this tube. See your body and aura filling with white healing light. The light represents your life force and divine pure love. It is the essence of everything and provides all that you ever need in the physical and all other aspects of your life. In this state, you have no fear. You are loved, secure, safe, happy and abundant. You can create what you need when you need it. Allow this energy to now pour into your body aura and mind. See yourself filled and surrounded with a constant source of light and love.

You can connect to the true Source at anytime to clear, guide and heal you. Practice connecting to the Source using this visualisation when ever you feel insecure, worried, or fearful in anyway.

Many fears stem from the misguided belief that you are disconnected from Universal Love. These thoughts feel bad because they invest you in believing that there is a lack of supply. Whether this is money, food, love, or time. By energetically reconnecting, you reassure yourself that you are always supplied and you are safe and loved. Use this energy as the basic element for everything manifest in your world, if you need more of anything then ask for and connect to this source this will renew your faith and help you to create all that you ever need.

LOVE is whom we really are without our ego behaviours, which come from...fear. When you connect to the Source of love, you eliminate the need for fear.

The following practices and techniques will help to prevent you from seeking energy from unhealthy sources. You will discover that you do not need to crave 'fixes' of energy because in truth you are always receiving all that you need. As you use these techniques, you clear away the negative beliefs and emotions that tie you to unhealthy addictive behaviours.

Learning these processes can help you to improve relationships especially where control and co-dependency are issues. They will also help you to be more self-aware and to manifest and receive all the supplies and items that you desire through the Law of Attraction. These energetic practices help you to more easily guide your thoughts and focus on the things you want to create.

Managing your aura

So many personal and health issues can be resolved by managing and recharging your life force energy through the auric field.

Unfortunately this knowledge is not widely available and negative habits can develop from early childhood because it is then that we may begin to feel that there is not enough love, energy or resources to go around. These fear-based habits are often called attention seeking in children and can take many forms that develop into toxic adult behaviours that negatively affect relationships, and emotional and physical health.

There are many unhealthy ways energy can be consciously or unconsciously taken from outside of you. During challenging times we can all experience depleted energy and seek a boost from outside sources. A bad habit can develop to grab energy from other people or addictive substances. It is not uncommon to eat chocolate or a have a caffeine fix when you hit mid afternoon fatigue. In times of stress or depression one person might smoke a cigarette or call a friend to complain, another might create an argument with their partner in an unconscious effort to find energy.

We have all experienced having our energy drained by someone else, perhaps you have someone in your life that is always complaining and feeling sorry for themselves. This can drain energy. At the end of a one-sided conversation you might feel depleted and depressed. This behaviour is easy to recognise in others, those that do it regularly are often called 'psychic vampires' and we learn to avoid them. The truth is that most people have taken energy from another person at some time or another and often it is unconscious. Although it is disconcerting to realise that you might have mistakenly drained another person, it's wonderful to have awareness and learn a new way to recharge your batteries.

Remember that this behaviour comes from fear and the mistaken thought that there is not enough energy, love or resources for you to live a full and happy life. When you reconnect to your true Source you are reminded that there is enough and as the healthy habit grows the universe reflects this new belief with solid evidence: not only will you feel better but you will begin to notice that you are attracting new loving people and situations into your life which support you.

There are several ways in which a person can attempt to recharge their energy from outside of themselves, usually the aura attaches in someway to a substance or person accompanied by some specific behaviours or signs. Remember your energy is for you and need only come from the Source, when you reach out to others you not only steal from them you are denying a part of your own life force and you cannot always guarantee what you are about to receive into your own energy field.

There are four major ways in which people seek energy I have named these behaviours; stuffing, hooking, draining and attaching for the ways in which the energy is taken into the auric field.
They all result in the same outcome; the energy field attaches itself to something or someone else in order to gain a short lived 'fix'.

Energy seeking behaviours

- **Stuffing:** Accompanying behaviours are overeating, binge drinking, lying, addictive shopping, drugtaking, and hoarding. This can be accompanied by an anxiety condition, which may cause the 'stuffer' to withdraw from social interactions. When it comes from an addiction or non-physical outlet, the energy gained from the food, drug or other items, pads or cushions the energy field and creates a block so that you can't feel fear or lack of vitality. People with weight issues are often subconsciously stuffing their auras in order to feel safe and energised. Once they learn to manage their energy they can more easily lose weight.

- **Attaching:** This is when you completely attach your aura like a conjoined twin to another energy field, particularly a lover or close family member. The dependant person seems to want to inhabit the other. It can be a two-way agreement as in co-dependant relationships where they feed off each other and feel like they can't exist apart. Each person is receiving some kind of 'pay off' for the relationship. The feeling of detachment can be painful and create dramatic arguments if one tries to leave or seems to not be giving adequate attention to another. Attaching can also occur through worry or obsessing about another, an arm of your energy field literally reaches out to the other person even if they are not in your vicinity. If you find yourself unable to let go or preoccupied with another person, then it's time to withdraw your energy and reconnect to the source.

- **Hooking:** Hooking occurs for those who have learned to command attention through behaviours such as yelling, tantrums, intellectual lectures or long monologues. They literally hook into other people's energy fields via the crown chakra at the top of the head whilst they have their attention. This can create headaches and confusion for the recipient.

- **Draining:** This is when you indiscriminately drain others with sad stories, illness, self-pity, and worry thoughts. These 'poor me' behaviours attach etheric tubes that suck energy from people. These ties or arms of energy can drain multiple people or individuals. The arm usually attaches into the solar plexus chakra above the naval and can leave you feeling empty, hollow or sore in that area.

It can be difficult to acknowledge that you sometimes behave this way; you have probably experienced being on the receiving end of someone else's draining behaviour! Learn this information and then let go of any guilt, judgement or resentment.

This energetic draining occurs because most people do not know another way and if they knew the other way they would behave differently. Most people are unaware so therefore deserve to be forgiven; no one deserves to be judged. Mistaken actions and thoughts just need a correction through learning another way.

The techniques offered further on will show you how to healthily replenish and stop bad habits! When you know better you can do better!

Unhealthy ways to replenish energy

- Constant complaining and self-pity (draining);
- Telling problems to anyone who will listen (draining);
- Cravings and addictions (stuffing);
- Over eating (stuffing);
- Commanding or demanding attention (attaching, hooking);
- Obsessing about relationships, objects, and money (attaching, draining, stuffing);
- Collecting or hoarding possessions (stuffing);
- Co dependency (draining, attaching);
- Neediness (draining, attaching);
- Insecurity and possessiveness (attaching);
- Directing anger (hooking);
- Lecturing (hooking);
- Stealing energy from others through non-stop talking (draining, hooking);
- Having constant dramas (draining, hooking);
- Lying (stuffing, draining, hooking);
- Blaming others (attaching, draining).

Taking another's life force energy leads to all kinds of unpleasant karma. Healthy people tend to avoid you and you will attract more negativity towards you in the form of other energy drainers. Unfortunately, as you take person's life force energy you can also end up with their negative energy as well. This is why co dependant relationships are so unpleasant and have big highs and lows! It is so much healthier and leads to more happiness and abundance to have your energy field only connected to the God Source and safely located around your own body.

Case study: Cindy

Cindy was a talented and very sensitive healer who had recently discovered her skills. Unfortunately she had not learned to control her energy and like many new healers thought it was okay to reach into another person's energy to 'read' them.

This is a popular misconception by intuitive people because they are so keen to help and heal others they jump in and have a 'feel' with their aura without permission. This can be as palpable as a physical arm touching your body to a sensitive person and is not on.

Cindy called a new friend on the phone and during the call sensed that her friend was very emotional, but being in the presence of her husband with whom she was arguing, Cindy's friend couldn't tell her story. Cindy reached into her friend's energy and immediately felt ill, angry and negative, exactly as her friend was feeling.

She was so shocked by the sudden intake of negative energy that she complained to her friend that her energy was 'disgusting' and had to put the phone down to recover.

The friend was upset by this and by the fact that her energy had just been intruded upon. This interaction could have been better handled by offering a healing and gaining permission to find out what was wrong.

A healthier way to Find energy

Once you determine the unhealthy ways you have been trying to manage and replenish your energy, you can correct your mistakes and easily reconnect to the Source. Forgive yourself for your mistakes by telling yourself the truth that you did not know better and understand that your ego fear was in charge, now you are taking your power back and placing your wellbeing into the hands of your loving higher self.

There are many healthy ways to replenish and clear your energy without losing your intuition and compassion. Once you try the methods described you will find your cravings for unhealthy substances and behaviours alleviates, and you will find it easier to quit if you want to. You may also find that you will attract less energy drainers because they cannot easily receive a 'fix' from you.

Healthy ways to replenish your energy:

- Connecting to the Source and managing your auric field using the visualisation and prayer on page 59.

- Sharing and processing thoughts and feelings with counsellors/therapists and loving friends.

- Meditation and prayer.

- Connecting to the angels and other loving spiritual beings.

- Releasing negative attachments.

- Healing past wounds.

- Following your passion.

- Allowing yourself to receive help from others.

- Spending time in nature.

- Exercise.

- Sleep and rest.

- Healthy eating and hydration.

- Energy healing such as Reiki or crystal healing.

- Loving and positive thoughts and actions.

- Self-responsibility.

- Creativity.

- Listening to music.

How your energy can leak

There can be many reasons for feeling drained and losing energy; including stress and worry. As you learned in the previous section your auric field can attach, hook or drain another, in an attempt to seek energy however your aura can also leak and send energy, losing precious life force.

For instance:

Worrying or obsessive thoughts can send an arm of your auric field out to the subject of your thoughts, sending and draining energy. All of your energy is pouring out towards the subject of worry, or obsession leaving you drained and single minded. The other person can also feel this energy and may also feel drained and distracted.

Scattered thinking creates a colander effect leaking out energy and life force from the aura. This can leave you feeling extremely fatigued and connected to lots of people and situations with arms or ties. These auras look frayed or like shock of hair spraying outwards. No energy is left for the person, and they look and feel frayed or scattered.

Angry venting can throw daggers of energy out to the subject of anger and anyone in the way. These people feel harsh to be around as they spew out anger. Their energy is sharp and toxic and they look that way too.

These behaviours have a draining and toxic effect on everyone concerned. The aura will absorb fear energy from what or whomever it connects with, which is then transferred into the physical body. These energy leaks come from worry and anger, yet they do nothing to resolve the fears. Instead they exacerbate the situations by creating more negativity. True to the Law of Attraction, like attracts like and the situation builds.

The life force goes wherever the aura goes, once the energy field is negatively directed towards another place or person this will create fatigue, confusion and an inability to detach from the behaviours and situations.

For instance:

When a needy person attaches to another, this normally creates an unhealthy co-dependent relationship or the other person senses this drain on their energy and becomes unobtainable.

A worried person will be so attached to the cause of their worries they cannot concentrate on any other thoughts. All of their energy is pouring outwards leaving them without a connection to their inner wisdom.

Someone obsessing over a past or present lover will be unable to let go of their feelings until they disconnect their arm of energy. All of their energy is with the other person and they can feel powerless to move on.

An angry person pushes people away from them and sends negative energy to the source of their anger, which does not resolve the problems or their feelings. They tend to attract more angry reactions in others and therefore perpetuate the cycle.

A scattered worrier is losing life force at such a pace that they are in danger of illness or mental confusion. They are actually attracting more situations to be worried about through the Law of Attraction.

These are not rewarding behaviours! However, most people behave this way without conscious knowledge of what they are doing!

You can learn to control and manage your energetic behaviour and this in turn can assist you in:

- Creating stronger boundaries;

- Higher vitality;

- Healthier relationships;

- Greater concentration and focus;

- Higher intuition and awareness;

- Healthier thoughts and intentions;

- Attracting more of what you want into your life via the Law of Attraction.

Changing the energetic behaviour assists in changing the unhealed thought processes and beliefs at the source of the behaviour. Once you reconnect to love you simultaneously attract all the things you want!

Unhealthy behaviours usually start at an early age. Some children many develop unhealthy behaviours in order to survive some difficult childhood situations. Sometimes children simply emulate or react against their parent's energy patterns. These behaviours become toxic in adult life as the need for childhood survival is replaced with a need to take responsibility and have happy healthy relationships. Self-forgiveness and self-awareness can help you to eliminate and replace unhealthy toxic habits.

A visualisation to manage your energy field

If you feel that you may be directing your energy in an unhealthy way then this visualisation and healing technique will return your auric field to its proper place. Once your aura surrounds you, you will begin to feel stronger, more energised and protected. This is the energetic equivalent of taking back your power! Practice these methods often to train your mind and energy to stay where you need them to.

Sit or lie in a quiet space where you will not be disturbed. Set the intention to know how your energy drains you and others.

Take three long deep breaths and empty your mind of thoughts. Visualise your aura either through your feelings or inner vision. Sense how big it is and its shape around your body. Slowly scan from your feet up to above your head. Notice any colours, blockages or unusual shapes. Let go of this information as you go.
Do not get too attached to your thoughts or interpretation.

Notice if you have any arms of energy reaching out from any part of you. Try to ascertain where these are reaching. Does this make sense for you? How have your thoughts and emotions been contributing to this situation?

Now let go again and think of someone whom you think about often. Focus on this person for a moment before bringing your attention to your energy field. What is happening?

You may have already intuitively understood if any of the unhealthy energy behaviours are relevant to you. A situation or relationship may have come to mind. Watch your aura again and ask for confirmation that you are losing or draining energy in this way.

Now intend to know how your energy behaves in your significant life situations, one at a time. Visualise your significant relationships, your work, any area where you might have difficulty, watch your aura, and note if it changes accordingly. You can learn a lot about yourself with this practice!

When you are ready to finish the meditation, take three more deep clearing breaths. Intend to release any mistaken thinking or beliefs that have created these patterns of behaviour.

Imagine that there is a bright beam of white and golden light around the outside of your body and aura, as you call your energy back towards you bring it through this beam of gold white light and imagine it cleansing.

Now consciously pull your energy back in towards you and bring it into shape around your body. Remove any arms or attachments of energy. Send the beam of white light through your entire aura and body to cleanse it.

Send a tree root of energy out from your feet and into the earth. Make the intention for you to receive all energy from God the Source.

Cover your aura with a shield of purple or blue light.

With your breath bring yourself back to awareness of the room and your surroundings.

Make notes in a journal about your discoveries.

It is useful to check in with your aura every so often, make sure it is not reaching out to others or frittering energy away. If you find yourself in a worrisome state of mind, healing your aura will heal your thoughts!

Abundance and your energy

Your energy has a direct impact on your prosperity and abundance in all other aspects of your life. Everything in our universe is made of energy and has a specific vibration. Money, goods and time are also forms of energy and will mirror the behaviour of your life force energy. Remember you control all the energy coming in and going out of your life, you control your thoughts; therefore your personal vibration and you control your auric field.

The phrase 'Like attracts like' is the basis for the Universal Law of Attraction. This means that for something to be attracted into your life it must match in vibration to the energy that you are emitting. Your vibration depends on your thoughts, words, behaviours, beliefs and emotions. Your auric field and energy is your vibration and behaves accordingly. In other words, what happens within your energy field is manifesting in your physical life in relationships, money, career and health right now.

When you learn about your energy you get an insight into your beliefs and unhealed aspects of yourself that may be attracting unwanted situations into your life. For example a leaky colander-like energy field of a worried, scattered person, will attract even more situations and people to worry about and can also mean that any prosperity that is attracted automatically seeps through their hands to others. If energy is lost or wasted then prosperity will follow the same pattern.

Drained feelings or lack of energy manifests as a lack of time, lack of abundance, lack of love and lack of helpful people. Similarly, a person who looks for energy from other people in order to feel satisfied can have financial and other lack issues. To them, it seems like the world is ungenerous and uncaring. The seeming shortage has caused them to beg, steal or borrow energy. They have not yet learned that energy comes from the Universal Source; it can come via other people but in a loving generous way. Those with a needy vibration never feel secure or fulfilled as their belief is in 'lack'.

To correct these issues pull your energy in and around you and reconnect to the Universal Source, the source of all that ever manifests. By doing this, you place yourself in the correct position to receive and keep all that you need and want without having to take it in unhealthy ways. As you begin to feel fulfilled, you are then able to give freely without fear.

A strong connected energy field with good boundaries creates a strong energised person with good boundaries who is able to receive all the abundance that is desired and share generously with others.

As you manage your energy using these simple visualisations, you automatically correct the mistaken fear beliefs that have caused the behaviour in the first place. As you heal your energy and thoughts, you raise your vibration, which begins to attract more of what you want into your reality.

Chapter 4

How to heal without being drained

Caring individuals radiate love and caring and therefore attract people who need and want healing. This can have a negative effect upon the carer who does not know how to manage their energy. Their empathy causes them to offer healing and perhaps take on the negativity or pain. They might entrain to or become drained by a needy person who is seeking a fix of positive energy.

So many people are depleted and seeking love and healing energy. There really is nothing to fear here. Energy can only be drained because loving sensitives want to help others but do not understand how to without giving their own energy away. Most healers think that they must give their energy. In truth, all they need to do is connect to the Source and ask for the Universal or God healing energy to be sent through the healer to the recipient. All healing energy must be channelled so that the healer is protected. Reiki healers are attuned to the Reiki healing energy and receive it through their bodies to their hands, passing it on to whomever they are healing. The word Reiki translated means universal life force.

Anyone can ask to be a channel of healing. You do not have to be a trained or attuned professional healer to access the energy because this Source is available to all.

I do recommend training if you intend to make healing a profession. Reiki and other modalities offer training, knowledge and support to the healer. However, as a caring sensitive you can ask to be protected and connected to the Source of love in any situation. Try it whilst listening to a distressed friend, intending healing to be sent to your pet, or saying a prayer for an ill relative in order to protect your own energy and add power to your intentions.

Another issue that carers and healers have is knowing what to do with the negative energy that is released when they assist someone; often the sensitive absorbs another person's painful feelings in an effort to heal them. This is a common mistake because they intuitively know they have to help remove the pain but they assume that they must take it on. In truth any released energy must be sent away to 'the light' or heaven where it can be cleansed and transformed into love energy. This process is called transmutation and you can call upon your guides and angels to do this for you.

When you find yourself giving healing through counselling, prayer or hands on healing to someone in need then use the following prayer to ensure you do not deplete your own precious life force or take on any released pain.

Dear God, angels, (any divine being that you would like to pray to)

I ask your assistance today to help to heal (name). Please make me a clear channel of divine healing and love; please connect me to the Source of healing energy so that all energy comes from you rather from my own energy. Guide my words and actions and please protect me from absorbing any negativity and transmute all released pain and fear to heaven for healing. Thank you, amen.

This is a very powerful prayer, when you ask heaven to assist you to be a channel of divine healing and love and help you to send any negative energy away to be transmuted elsewhere, you completely protect yourself from being drained and absorbing fear based emotions. You source the healing from heaven rather than your own energy and you allow divine energy to work through you.

Permission to heal

Remember to always ask permission to heal another and if you don't have permission, prayer is a wonderful and powerful way to enlist divine help and invoke the highest good for another without intruding upon another person's energy and privacy. Sometimes a healer's ego takes over and results in an unasked for intervention to heal another persons pain, some healers gain a sense of superiority from this behaviour, which can have an un-healing effect on all concerned.

Allowing yourself to receive

Giving and receiving of energy should always be in balance. When the energy out outweighs energy in it will create an imbalance in the form of resentment and seeming lack. When the reverse is true, it will create blockages such as guilt or dissatisfaction. Without awareness sensitive givers and healers can become trapped in a cycle of over giving, resentment and exhaustion. To exacerbate this you can become overly focussed on giving and nurturing, making it a part of your identity and self-esteem. A low self-worth feeds the need to care and give, which creates unhealthy relationships. The consequent ties and toxic energy block the love energy sending you further into fear.

Sensitive's often do not reach out when they need help because they know how it feels to be drained and they fear sapping other people's energy. Consequently, these givers find it hard to receive and become unbalanced.

True to the Law of Attraction, the illusion of lack increases and effects finances and relationships. A sign that you are in a cycle of over giving or not managing energy correctly is that you feel often exhausted, broke and used.

A way to correct this is to allow yourself to receive — if this is difficult ask yourself why. There is a lesson here in self worth and healing for misguided beliefs. To keep in balance and allow a natural flow of energy you must allow yourself to receive help, healing and material wealth, give yourself rest time, good food, and self-care. It always amazes me how many givers seem averse to receiving gifts, and will always put themselves last.

You may have negative feelings about receiving money for your time and energy; this comes from fears about worthiness and feeling unqualified or even guilty. If you have a passion to heal and send love to the world then your intention can create miracles in your life and in the lives of others if you let it. You may well be guided to gain qualifications in a certain modality; you might just need practice and confidence to use your God given gifts. However it is a mistake to undervalue your time and energy. If you struggle with charging for your skills then place the value on your time instead. Your beliefs always manifest in the physical world if you believe you are unworthy then you will create situations that mirror this belief.

It is self-responsible to recognise your own needs and find healthy ways to fulfil them before assisting others. It is irresponsible to believe that you must fix the world and exhaust yourself in the process. All energy is paid forward. Fear, if not managed properly, will pass on as surely as love and inspiring energy radiates. Seek to leave love wherever you go. It starts with you!

How to give without being drained

- Recognise that there is an unlimited Source of energy available to all and that healing energy comes through, not from the healer.

- Remember keep your ego in check: your client or friend may have just forgotten how to connect to this Source. Any judgement or negativity from you will lower your own energy and add to the fear of the person you are helping.

- Protect and ground your energy using one of the methods in the following chapter.

- Check that your aura is in place and not reaching out to or intruding upon the other person.

- Know that all pain/fear is an illusion and that in truth all is well.

- Pray for assistance from God and the angels and ask for the energy required to counsel or talk with the person to come from the Source rather than your own energy.

- Ask that all released pain and fear is transmuted to the light, so that you do not absorb it.

- Ask the angels to help all concerned to understand that everyone has all the power with in them to heal him or herself.

- When you leave, disconnect any ties or arms of energy between you to detach and clear yourself.

Managing energetic intrusions

You have learned that your energy can feel low or drained when you detach from the Source and try to send or take energy from other sources; you can also feel low energy as you entrain to another person's vibration. However there are other ways in which your energy can be negatively affected. These situations happen when outside energy encroaches upon your very sensitive and open energy.

As a sensitive you will have experienced feeling overwhelmed, fatigued, drained, emotional and stressed for no apparent reason. As you become more tuned in, you will learn that there is always a reason and with the awareness you can begin to apply the practices offered here to protect your precious energy.

Sensitive energy can be like a sponge that absorbs or takes on the negative energy from people as well as places and property.

The energy of locations

Visiting a crowded place can leave you feeling scattered, drained and even physically ill depending on the location. This is because the location is filled with lots of energy, which can influence, or even attach to, a sensitive person.

For instance, I cannot endure second hand or antique shops – because I can sense all the energy connected to all the previous owners! Often those who cannot let go haunt buildings and even stay attached to precious items that they loved in life! The energy of second hand shops can make me feel faint, ill and scattered.

Similarly, some homes, public places, patches of highway or road have Earth-bound spirits or energetic imprints from conflict, accidents or trauma that has occurred there.

A sensitive can feel these energies and may experience the negative emotions of the situation that occurred there. Common feelings in situations like these include:

- A strong pulling sensation;

- Air pressure or temperature changes;

- Nausea;

- A physical tightness such as a choking sensation;

- Headaches.

I feel my throat tighten and nauseous when I encounter Earth-bound spirits or haunted areas.

Emotional energy

An afternoon with a depressed friend can leave you feeling low and drained for many days; a lifetime of working as a counsellor or in another service industry can cause a build up of 'ties' and toxic energy which can create havoc with your body, mind and emotions if you do not know how to clear them. This is one reason why there is a high burnout rate in the industry of welfare and community services. The loving individuals who are attracted to help others become literally bogged down with all the sadness and pain that they encounter.

Empathic people have a subconscious tendency to absorb the pain from others; without awareness this can be disastrous. This can even happen in a public place if an ill or needy person passes you by. Many sensitives who have experienced this have told me that they will not work as healers for this reason.

There are several ways in which outside energy can affect your energy:

- The negative energy of a place or person/s passes into the energy of a sensitive leaving them feeling unwell, heavy and confused. The negative energy has to be cleared or released.

- Busy areas such as shopping centres, airports and hospitals contain a lot of energy including earth-bound spirits and trapped emotional energy which can negatively absorb or attach to your aura.

- In close proximity, emotional and physical feelings from others can be sensed and unconsciously taken on. Many sensitives feel confused about whether an emotional feeling is their own or that of another person – especially in close relationships.

- Unwelcome attachments and emotions can come from earth bound spirits and entities. These beings act a bit like energetic leeches, they latch on to light filled beings in order to charge up their own energy. Earthbound spirits might be attracted to someone in the hope that they could communicate a message. These beings tend to prevail in places where there is a history of tragedy, pain or addictions such as in bars, hospitals or massacre sites.

- A needy or insecure person can attach their energy to yours in order to feel better. These people can get quite angry if their source is removed.

- You can have tie attachments created through your own fearful thoughts and feelings of another. For example, anger at your partner can cause a tie attachment passing toxic energy between you.

- Lost Earth-bound spirits in your home or in public areas can have a negative influence on sensitive individuals. Children can be particularly affected. The spirits are often feeling angry, confused or sad. Their strong emotions seep into the area and those who live there. It is important to treat these individuals with compassion, try to understand how terrifying it feels to be lost and suddenly invisible to most people. Call upon the Archangel Michael to clear the area and take the spirit to the light.

- You might have experienced having your energy taken by unhappy or needy living people who cannot seem to fill themselves up. The feeling is akin to someone taking a straw and sucking all the energy out of you, there may be a feeling of emptiness or soreness around your solar plexus area, which is a good indication that this person has 'plugged in'.

- Energy can also disappear because you are allowing it to just fritter away in an uncontrolled way with scattered thoughts, over giving, stress and emotional rollercoasters.

- Entrainment: Negative thoughts and complaints will seem to deplete energy because the negative vibrating emotions are of a lower vibration. The feeling of lowering your vibration to match these thoughts creates the sensation of losing energy when in fact you are attracting more negativity and darkening your own energy field. This can happen when you encounter negative thinking people as your vibration begins to match theirs.

- Environmental pollutants such as electromagnetic waves from electronic equipment also affect energy sensitive people, as does working under false lighting, and radiation from screens. Try to spend as much time as possible outdoors to counteract the negative effects and clear your energy. Drinking water will help; use certain crystals such as smoky quartz in front of your computer screen to form an energetic barrier.

Whatever the reason for feeling drained or low in energy, the effects can be confusing and it can become hard to stay focussed and centred. This is when it is doubly important to be conscious of your auric field and body.

These effects are not to be feared but good awareness and firm management are definitely required. It is important not to judge or label friends and family who may unwittingly drain you. Be compassionate, often people do not realise they are doing this and just notice they feel better after spending time with you.

Thank them for teaching you this valuable lesson and then learn to manage and protect your own energy so that you can still be compassionate with clear boundaries. As you become stronger in your own energy you will be able to more easily lift people's vibrations. They will entrain to you rather than the other way around. Then you will have no need to look for unhealthy methods to regain your own energy.

Addictions

When it all gets too much it is common to turn to addictions for solace and protection, such as eating, smoking, sugar, caffeine, antidepressants, computer games, alcohol, gambling, drugs and certain emotional states.

Addictions represent an outside search for energy. When you feel depleted, you might seek an energetic high from an outside source. It is common to reach for a chocolate bar and a cup of tea when you hit a mid-afternoon low! You can crave romance, attention, drugs or an adrenalin rush for the same reason.

Addictive substances work to suppress emotional and physical pain and therefore numb or turn off your sensitivity. Certain substances create a layer of dense energy such as smoke around the body and aura much like a shield. This might sound useful, but unfortunately, unhealthy energy blocks the intuition and life force and is detrimental to the energetic and physical body. Toxic substances create lumps of dark energy with in the aura, which block the flow of positive energy. Over time these blocks can manifest within the physical body.

Here are some physical, emotional and spiritual side effects from unhealthy addictions and cravings that I have discovered:

- Sugar blocks the third eye chakra, your centre for wisdom and intuition found between your eyebrows. This can be indicated by a headache or tired eyes and accompanied with a shut down of the intuitive processes and inner wisdom.

- Sugars and additives stimulate irritation, anger and unhappiness. They can be the source of hyperactive behaviour in children.

- Drugs create torn and frayed energy fields filled with psychic dirt, which attract entities and other negative situations.

- Over eating can create a layer of unhealthy fat around the body. Often sensitives struggle with weight because they give so much to others. This layer represents a need to be protected.

- Smoking causes a choking effect on the aura, in the form of a grey/brown cloud, which can block receptivity, including psychic communication and lowers the energetic vibration.

- Marijuana smoke creates a dull brown aura. Smokers often have communication and heart chakra issues including unhealed grief which later manifest in the physical heart and lungs.

- Addictions deplete energy after the initial false 'high' because the real need for life force energy has not been met.

- Addictions exacerbate the illusion of fear and the mindset of 'lack' because the addict is always looking for more from outside of themselves often attaching to other energy fields.

- The toxic energy created by unhealthy addictions and the ties to the subject of addiction creates coagulated dark energy within the body and energy field and unhealed emotional blocks.

- Stimulants such as caffeine create nervousness, anxiety and hyperactive behaviour in sensitive adults and children. This includes uncontrolled negative thinking and colander-like energy leaks.

- Addictive behaviour lowers the self-esteem of the addict because they feel controlled by their needs and they know in their hearts it is destructive or unhealthy. They can never satisfy their true need in this way and are trapped in a cycle.

Sensitive young people and children are commonly drawn to addictive behaviours. They feel the need to escape the pain of the world around them. Unfortunately, the desensitisation and the added low vibrations of the chosen addiction can manifest as physical and emotional disorders for these highly sensitive beings. Allergies, intolerances, mysterious pain, behavioural disorders and suppressed emotions are amongst the problems that manifest. Once they begin to tune into their sensitivity and protect their energy, they can heal their addictions and any disorders.

Case study: Brydey

Brydey has been challenged with sensitivity since early childhood. She tells of hearing spirit voices and seeing visions at aged four and was plagued with reoccurring illness. She is sensitive to toxins in foods, drugs, alcohol, pollutants, crowds, negative emotion in other people, and spirit activity. She has had a long challenge maintaining her energy levels and keeping her aura around her.

Her clairvoyance allows her to detect dark intentions and drug abuse in people's auras in the form of green/yellow tinges and what she calls 'etheric snot'. Brydey says she 'always felt different and 'mistakenly thought there was something wrong with me and just wanted to die.'

These feelings are very common in a sensitive. She had no protection for her extreme sensitivity and to deal with stress would 'detach and flip out of [her] body'. Her aura would spread outward to everyone she thought about so her precious life force was leaking. She has always been passionate about protecting the environment and is highly creative but was steered away from these pursuits by well meaning adults in favour of more mainstream studies and work.

The struggles with pain, depression, and illness, whilst trying to override her natural tendencies created an intense depression in early adulthood; Brydey turned to drug use to cope, which culminated in a misdiagnosis of psychosis, a mental illness. Finally she was guided to learn about her sensitivity and how to manage it.

Today Brydey is a mother and leads a spiritually based, healthy lifestyle she has learned to eat healthily, manage negativity, pollutants and toxins and apply clearing, shielding and grounding techniques to cope with her sensitivity which she now recognises as a gift.

Healing addictions

Addictive behaviours can be healed when you learn to manage and protect your sensitive energy. If you consistently pull in your aura and realign yourself to the Source, you will find that your cravings fade away as you withdraw energy from the outside source.

When you are addicted to a substance or behaviour, you form energetic attachments to the addiction. This is because you your addictions represent a search for energy, a replacement for divine love. The negative attachment is toxic and controlling. When you release this tie you can reconnect to the truth about where love and energy really comes from.

Toxins, diet and the Sensitive person

Diet is very important for sensitive people. As you honour your sensitivity, you will find that you become even more sensitive to foods and beverages because you can actually now hear the messages that your body has been telling you all along. For instance when I began to eat a cleaner diet I found I could no longer tolerate caffeine and other toxins.

My body began to steer me away from unhealthy substances. Many sensitives already know that they have intolerances and allergies to certain foods and beverages.

Case study: Michelle

'I suffered much sensitivity to foods; especially the more processed ones and often had anxiety and panic attacks. Being in crowds was unbearable as the energy was so overwhelming. Living out of town (on a rural property) helps me to heal, cleanse and centre myself. Regular meditation and asking guidance to steer me in the right direction is essential, as are healthy food, fresh air and exercise.'

Case study: Heather

'I was living in Sydney. I had a lot of health problems due to the pollution in the area. I lost my sense of taste and always felt cloudy in my thoughts. My connection with the universe seemed weak as a result. Eight years later saw a move to the Mid North Coast where I started to see a naturopath who cleansed and detoxified my system, altered my diet and provided me with many healing sessions.

Through receiving crystal, drum, angel healings and being strict with my diet, messages started to become clearer and my spirituality continuously got stronger and stronger. I armed myself with tools to be able to stay grounded and focussed on service.'

Your goal as a sensitive person is to feel energised, healthy and to have a clear mind and intuition. This involves detoxifying your body. The release of toxins will also clear up many lower vibrating emotions. Depression, hyperactivity, low concentration, and emotional highs and lows have been linked to certain ingredients in food and beverages. On the journey for more clarity and joy, you will undoubtedly receive some guidance to clean up your diet.

Here are some of the common items that block and inhibit intuition and create mood changes:

- Sugar, including corn syrups and other products;*
- Chocolate;
- Alcohol, including wine;
- Smoking;
- Caffeine, particularly in coffee;
- Dairy products;*
- Processed foods;
- Wheat products;*
- White breads;
- Meat;*
- Excessive salt;*
- Strong chemical cleaning products;
- Perfumes, moisturisers and shampoos with harsh chemicals in them;
- Tooth pastes with chemicals;
- Marijuana;
- Electromagnetic vibration – from computers and other devices.

*Often these ingredients are consumed in excess, which creates the problem; please consult your health professional before making any extreme diet changes and for nutritional advice.

When the subject of dietary toxins comes up during a reading, usually my clients have already received some guidance that these have a negative affect on them. They will say something like, "Ooh I have noticed lately that my morning coffee has been giving me palpitations or makes me feel unwell."

It is common to crave chocolate even though it blocks the intuition. This can be an unconscious act of self-sabotage due to fears about being clairvoyant. These fears are linked to a desire for social acceptance and some people have past life memories where they were punished for having 'witch-like' skills. These skills included herbal medicine, energy healing, intuitive readings and homeopathy.

The guidance that something is unhealthy for your body and aura will come through physical and emotional signals. If you ignore these symptoms they will worsen to give you a louder warning.

Not everything listed above is unhealthy, if consumed or exposed to in moderation. Obviously, harsh chemicals, drugs and cigarette smoke are toxic for everyone, sensitive or not. A sign that you are becoming increasingly sensitive is that you will start to have intolerances to toxic and unhealthy substances. As you begin to alter your lifestyle you can balance some activities, such as working under false lighting or with computers, by spending time outdoors each day and by using the clearing methods described in the following chapter.

Sometimes those on a spiritual path find that they are attracted to becoming a vegetarian or vegan. This was true for me as my intuition opened up. I was immediately turned off meat and began to crave fresh juices and salads. It is important to balance any diet with correct amounts of protein, carbohydrates and vitamins. If you feel guided to change to a vegetarian or vegan diet, make sure you get up to date professional information about eating a balanced healthy diet.

An ideal diet is that of fresh organic foods with plenty of clean water. You can even keep a food diary for a week where you write down what you eat and how you feel after it. After a while, you will find that you are more attracted to foods that support your sensitivity and intuition.

Chapter 5

Clearing, grounding and protecting your energy

To honour your sensitivity, hear your intuition and healthily cope with life your energy needs to be regularly cleared, grounded and protected.

Clearing means that your energy and body are swept clean of all negative energy and attachments.

Grounding means that you are centred in your physical body and earthed. Many sensitives tend to psychically and energetically detach from their physical bodies as a way of coping – this can lead to a scattered, vague mind and also be very dangerous. Have you ever driven your car somewhere and wondered how you got there? If so, you were ungrounded.

Shielding provides a 'buffer' of protection for your physical emotional and auric bodies. This prevents the sponge effect from taking place so you can be around negativity without absorbing it.

A shield also helps to prevent your energy from being drained away. Shielding provides you with a filter for negative energy and allows you to keep your life force energy on the inside. You can give your attention and healing energy, which comes from the divine infinite Source, to others endlessly without giving away your own energy and becoming drained.

Once cleared, grounded and shielded you will more easily hear your intuitive guidance because you will no longer be confused by all the other incoming energy of the world around you. You will also have more vital life force energy for yourself because it won't drain out to everyone you encounter.

Signs that your energy requires clearing, protection and grounding:

- Feeling drained of all energy;*

- Feeling unwell in particular places or situations;

- Craving caffeine, sugar and other pick me ups;

- Over eating or forgetting to eat;

- Feeling weepy or emotional for no apparent reason;

- Highs and lows in emotion;

- Attracting draining persons;

- Regular contact with depressed or dysfunctional people;

- Thinking about problems late at night;

- Feeling light headed, airy or faint;*

- Having difficulty concentrating on one task at a time;

- Feeling hungry or empty when you have eaten;

- Feeling shaky;*

- Feeling scattered;

- Leaving the room – not being in your body;

- A cluttered mind;

- Physical aches and pains;*

- Headaches;*
- Dazed eyes;*

- Spending too much time thinking, analysing and worrying;

- Feeling as if you have been punched in the stomach, or you have a neck or back ache after being with a particular person;

- Regular physical symptoms with no other cause e.g. nausea or fatigue;*

- Difficulty making decisions.

* Note: Always consult a medical professional about reoccurring physical symptoms.

Remember your physical and emotional feelings are a signal from your internal guidance system, so to truly honour your self you need to listen to what your feelings are telling you.

Energy clearing

You will feel so much more vital, free and confident when you clear your energy regularly. You will begin to understand how much energy you actually take on and how this affects you.

After a long day or when you are feeling drained or overwhelmed it is important to get rid of the negative energy that you may have accumulated, particularly if you are in contact with a lot of people, working under false lighting or near computers.

Some professions will take on energy into their physical body more easily, especially if the worker touches the client such as in massage therapy, nursing, hairdressing and beauty. Other professions such as counsellors and welfare workers who hear about people's problems all day long definitely need to clear their emotional and physical energy frequently. Supermarket checkout operators or people who work where there are a lot of passing customers will also benefit.

Light clearing method

Sit in a quiet spot and take a few deep breaths.

Close your eyes if you wish.

Call upon your angels, particularly Archangel Michael (the protector angel) and ask them to help you to clear your body and energy of all negative and dark energy, which might be draining you.

Imagine a bright white bubble of light around your whole body. Allow this light to pass in through the top of your head, filling your entire body and dissolving all negative energy. Allow this light to fill your aura. Breathe deeply, feel a ball of this light in the palm of each hand and flushing up through your wrists and arms.

When you feel that this light has filled your entire body, silently ask Archangel Michael to clear you of any dark energy or attachments. Breathe deeply as he works on you, clearing away all the toxins that he finds, release the negativity through your breath.

If there is a particular issue or person that you know is affecting your energy then tell the angel that you wish to release all negative ties related to (name). Be willing to let go of all of your uncomfortable feelings about this person including resentment and irritation. Breathe out these feelings and if you want, imagine sending love in the form of pink light.

You may feel a slight breeze or goose bumps as Archangel Michael moves over your body. Stay in position with your loving intentions until you sense that the healing is over.

You will feel lighter and clearer afterwards.

Thank Archangel Michael and your guardian angels for their healing.

Chakra clearing with the Mermaids

The ocean is a powerful natural healer. The fresh salt air and elements of nature easily penetrate the auric field and help to release negative energy.

The following meditation uses a visualisation of the ocean to clear the major chakras. Chakras are the centres, which process life force energy through our physical and etheric bodies. Chakras act like pumps similar to the heart: energy is sent and received via these centres that sit at appropriate points of the body. Each chakra also has a specific purpose related to a life area and colour.

Chakras, like your energy field, can become clogged or damaged with negative energy and behaviours. They need to be clear to process the energy up and down the body and to assist with clear intuition and connection. Clearing them is a precise way of clearing your energy and helps you to identify major blocks in your life. This process is a great way to heighten your intuition as it literally 'tunes you in'.

Here is a list of the major chakras, their associated life area and colour. As you visualise them it is helpful to see or sense them as a circle or ball of light about the size of a compact disc.

- Crown Chakra – purple and white light – this chakra is located at the top of the head and is related to divine and spiritual wisdom.

- Third eye or brow chakra—indigo light—the brow chakra is connected to inner wisdom and spiritual sight.

- Throat chakra – blue light – the throat centre is all about communication, creativity and self-expression.

- Heart Chakra – green light – the heart is the centre of universal, personal and romantic love.

- Solar plexus Chakra – golden light – your solar plexus is concerned with your will power and boundaries.

- Sacral Chakra – orange light – this is the centre of your emotions.

- Base Chakra – red light – this is the chakra concerned with the basics of life: sexuality, financial and personal security, and physical grounding.

If a chakra is dulled or misshapen it is because something is off balance in the particular life area. For instance, worries about the supply of money will produce blocks in the base chakra. A blockage in this area actually prevents the money from flowing to you. When a chakra is returned to its clear state it will heal mistaken thinking and help to attract the desired state, such as financial security. Chakras are just like your auric field: Thoughts, experiences and beliefs will create blocks. Beliefs about religion, love, self esteem or safety will affect the relevant chakra and clearing the chakra will help to heal the situation that created the block.

Cleansing your major chakras

This is a simple fun visualisation to cleanse your major chakras and energy field. It is even more effective when done at the beach!

Sit or lie quietly with your back straight, take several deep breaths to clear your mind.

Imagine that you are seated beside a blue ocean, it is a sunny clear day and the waves lap gently nearby.

You decide to walk into the warm water up to your waist, as you enjoy the experience, a beautiful mermaid surfaces beside you with long wavy hair decorated with sparkling gems and coral. She holds up a large conical shell and offers you a marine healing for your energy.

You agree and the mermaid takes your hand, you feel very safe. You are instantly transported to a large sheltered rock pool. The water is clear, coloured corals and sea creatures adorn the floor; you are seated at the edge on a smooth rock shelf in waist deep water, your mermaid is in front of you. Holding her conical shell above your head, she begins pouring a light filled golden green liquid over your entire body. As this liquid touches your skin, you feel instant warmth and relaxation flowing down from head to toe.

She waves her hand over the top of your head and then pours the light filled fluid again, this time into your body. You feel its calming clearing effect seeping through your head. In your mind's eye, you see and feel your crown chakra, being polished and brightened by this golden green liquid. All dark patches are instantly dissolved and you feel the energy flowing easily as the crown chakra glows a bright purple.

Now the water reaches your brow chakra between your eyebrows and again effortlessly cleanses away blocks, becoming sparkling indigo. On it flows into your throat melting dark energy until all that remains is a bright blue ball of light. Feel the loving energy as the magical mermaid pours healing elixir into your heart chakra, in the centre of your chest, brightening and healing your heart until it shines like an emerald.

Your solar plexus chakra is next to receive the purifying liquid and easily glows yellow gold activating your personal power centre. Next, it is poured over your sacral chakra below your naval until it becomes a bright orange colour, relaxing your emotions.

You feel wonderfully content and relaxed as the light filled fluid flows over the bright red chakra at the base of your spine, cleansing away all the negativity related to your material and physical being. As this occurs you feel a warming sensation as your base chakra sends energy down your lower body and out the sole of each foot. The energy looks like plant roots and penetrates the rocky pool floor spreading into the earth, securing and grounding your energy.

The mermaid asks you to hold out your hands and as she pours the liquid over the palms and fingers, you feel a tingling sensation as all the tiny chakras are activated.

Finally, she invites you into the pool and as you take a deep breath and dive beneath the surface you feel instantly charged with powerful healing energy. The mermaid shows you a row of coloured starfish and asks you to choose one for your protective shield colour. You are attracted to one and she waves it over you surrounding your bright clean energy field with a thin shell of your chosen colour to preserve the clarity and protect you from absorbing harmful energy.

There are many natural ways to clear and heal our energy some of the most effective involve being outside in nature. Everyone feels good after a walk on the beach or a day in the garden. One reason for this is that the healing elements of nature and the angels can effortlessly clear our energy.

Sunshine and moonlight are essential for spiritual, physical and emotional health and as long as you do not overdo it, this natural light will dissolve away negative energy.

Water is cleansing on all levels, a swim or bath in fresh or salt water will leave your energy sparkling. Make sure to drink adequate amounts of fresh pure water each day. As you advance on your spiritual path and honour your sensitivity, you may find that your water requirement increases.

Crystals have energy which they pass on to the user so a clearing or protective crystal can definitely help. Remember that like people, crystals need clearing regularly too.

Cleansing herbs like sandalwood and sage can smudge away negative energy from a room or person when they are burnt nearby. Allow the herbs to smoulder and waft the smoke around the area that needs clearing.

Have you noticed that you hold your breath or become short of breath in times of stress? Consciously taking deep slow breaths will clear your energy and help your body by oxygenating muscles and your brain.

Exercising outside is a superb way to cleanse and detoxify.

Music has magical elements that can clear away fear and uplift or heal the listener. Be selective and notice how different types of music affect your energy.

Meditation is the practice of clearing the mind and connecting to the divine and your higher self. Regular meditation will clear you and raise your vibration.

Prayer is one of the most powerful ways to clear and lift your energy — particularly if you feel you have absorbed or attracted some lower energy. Pray to God, the Archangel Michael and your guardian angels to protect and clear you and lift away toxic and negative intrusions from your mind, body and energies. Call upon your angels to lead you to gentler and lighter situations and to show you any guidance that you need to know to protect and honour your sensitivity. Prayer is the perfect way to clear away all lower energies including entities.

Once your energy is clear, you are ready to shield and ground.

Grounding your energy

Grounding means to be energetically located with in your physical body and connected to the earth. Ungroundedness occurs when you disconnect from awareness of the physical body and are not present; you sort of float half-in, half-out of your body and lose focus.

It is important to be present and grounded in your physical body whilst remaining connected to your higher self. Your physical body is as important as your energetic body. You have incarnated in material reality on earth for a physical and spiritual purpose.

Your body has a language and energy of its own and speaks to you through your senses; your physical form makes your intentions and actions real. Even if your purpose is spiritual healing, you still have to be here and connected to your body to do it. You can experience great joy through mother earth and your physical reality.

It is common for sensitives to not want to be grounded because of a fear of losing your connection to heaven and spirit. You may even enjoy the disconnection, which is like a floaty high at times. I believe this is because many of us remember and long for our spirit bodies that we experienced before each lifetime.

Sensitive people have also learned to disconnect as a way of disassociating from strong emotions, pain and intuitive signals. This coping mechanism actually works against you, sabotaging goals and projects because it is so easy to become distracted.

When you are ungrounded you can feel very confused, scattered and even shaky. When you are grounded you gain more control and a stronger connection to angels and spirit. Your intuition is like a radio picking up a signal; when you are ungrounded; the signal is fuzzy and picks up too much interference. Your intuition will be stronger and you will be more confident and clear when you practice grounding methods.

Grounding methods

The process of grounding is very simple and need only take a few minutes. You can vary the following methods or make up your own. The purpose is to connect your energy to the earth and be aware of your energy within your body.

1. Sit quietly on a chair or cross-legged on the floor. Ensure your back is straight and your tailbone is touching the floor or chair. Call in your guardian angels for help and then with eyes open or closed take a few deep breaths and focus inwards.

Become aware of your body, starting with your head, feel the energy within your head and neck, move or stretch them and breath, move your attention to your shoulders and chest, arms and hands, stomach and back, hips, pelvis, and legs and finally your feet. Tense or stretch each part and then focus on what it feels like inside each of this body part. You may detect tingling, warmth or pulsing. Now feel the entire body, really be inside your body for a few moments.

Bring your attention to your tailbone area that connects with the seat or floor.

Visualise a column or a tree root reaching from this area at the base of your spine and going deep into the earth. I like to make the grounding root a distinct colour — I choose red to match the base chakra energy or green for healing.Send the root far into Mother Earth and imagine that it meets a beautiful boulder of crystal in the depths of the earth. Wrap the arms of the root around the boulder. In this moment, you might feel warmth or an intuitive signal that you have grounded.

Take a deep breath and imagine all heaviness leaving your body and emotions through the root.

See all your worries, tensions, and fears travelling into the earth to be transmuted and healed.

2. Sit on a chair with your feet flat on the ground and your spine straight. Place your open palms on your lap and relax. Take three deep slow breathes. Visualise roots growing from your feet, travelling into the earth, and going deeper and deeper until they reach a bright red boulder in the centre of the earth wrap your roots around this boulder and feel the connection. Allow all your fears and negativity to leave your body and travel down the roots and into mother earth where they will be transmuted.

3. Sit or lie with your back straight, practice the chakra clearing method in the energy clearing section. When you reach the root chakra at the base of your spine, send the red energy down through your hips and into each leg, feel the energy travelling through your legs to the soles of your feet. Send the energy through the soles and down into the earth, spread these roots outwards, imagine them to be the roots of an old tree, spread them wide and deep giving you a secure grounding.

4. Lie comfortably on the floor with your back straight and legs hip width apart. Begin to focus on your breath. Relax and ask the angels to help cleanse and ground you. Visualise an angel at your feet and another at your head.

Now feel the angel at the top of your body send healing energy through the top of your head and down through your entire body. Feel it flowing like a waterfall into each cell, bone, muscle, follow it through your head, face, neck, throat, chest, upper back, relaxing and healing as it goes. Allow it to fill your arms, hands and fingers. Breathe deeply and allow this gently flowing light to enter your lower body, stomach, hips, buttocks, legs and finally to your feet.

When the light reaches your feet send a beam of this light out from the sole of each foot, the angel at your feet, grasps each beam *of light as if it is a rope and pulls it through, directing it to the ground, your angel pulls at the light ropes and brings them deeper and deeper into the earth. Finding a boulder the angel wraps your grounding rope around the boulder and returns to your feet. Feel the energy continuing through the top of your head and channelling into your body and into the earth.*

Take a few deep breaths, thank your angels and bring your awareness to your body laying on the surface, make note of each body part, either wiggling or tensing your muscles: Check in with the room, listen to the noises, feel the temperature. When you feel ready and fully aware sit up and drink some water.

Quick fixes for when you feel ungrounded:

- Take some deep cleansing breaths and call in the angels to ground you;

- Stand out doors with your bare feet on the earth or grass;

- Eat a raw carrot or other vegetable that grows beneath the earth;

- Massage the soles of your feet;

- Drink plenty of water;

- Have a massage;

- Stamp your feet;

- Exercise/stretch – or do some yoga;

- Ensure you have breaks in natural light when working on computers or under fluoro lighting;

- Name items in your vicinity aloud or mentally: e.g. 'lamp, desk, and fan';

- Carry hematite or smoky quartz, which are grounding crystals.

- If you have a tendency to prefer being ungrounded, I suggest grounding regularly through the day.

Shielding

Protecting your energy with light shield will prevent you from taking on unwanted energy into your body and energy field.

A shield is like a bubble or column of light surrounding you and your aura. It transmutes away negativity and protects you from physical, emotional and psychic harm. It is a barrier.

You will still be able to help others, empathise, hear your intuition and feel all the emotions you just will not retain any negativity or pain associated with outside situations and you won't be drained.

You will have more energy to fulfil all your responsibilities and work.

A good light shield prevents your energy from travelling away from you, it stops others being able to tap into your energy and drain you whilst still allowing you to help from a place of love. You will also prevent yourself from feeling other people's negativity and emotions, which can be draining, confusing and tiring.

If you massage or counsel people, you may notice that you pick up the pain or emotions of other people. Shielding will stop this from happening and you will not retain the pain or negative energy, which can cause burnout over long periods.

I suggest that you shield each morning. For stressful jobs, it is a great idea to re-shield between clients or before stressful situations. It is a great idea to do this after clearing and grounding your energy. Visualising the shield isn't necessary just asking your angels for the protection will ensure that it is done.

Suggested prayer to the angels for shielding

Dear Angels, please give me a shield of purple light (choose whatever colour suits your situation, see list below) that surrounds and protects me from head to toe, connects me to heaven and grounds me to mother earth. Lets in only what is for my highest good and lets out that which is not and transmutes all fear and negativity away for healing. Thank you and amen.

Shielding visualisation 1: The column

- Sitting or standing, take some deep breaths.

- Imagine you are inside a column of light, which flows down from above and surrounds your entire aura and body. All negativity bounces off or dissolves upon contact with this shield. See it covering you from head to toe. When you are satisfied you are surrounded with this light then you are shielded.

Shielding visualisation 2: The cleansing, shielding and grounding bubble

Sitting or standing with your spine straight. Take some deep breaths and focus within.

Visualise a column of bright white light coming from above your head and surrounding your entire body, imagine the light entering your body through the top of your head at the crown chakra, clearing and relaxing as it goes. Feel the light filling your head, travelling down through your face and into your throat and neck. Breathe and relax as it travels into your chest and around your lungs and heart. Allow the light to spread into each shoulder and down your arms, from the upper arm to the elbow, forearm and wrists, each muscle and bone, unwinding and relaxing, the tension flowing away. Your hands are warming with the light as it spreads from the palm into each fingertip.

The light continues to pour in from the top of your head. Feel it travelling gently down your neck to your spine and spreading outwards to all of your back muscles as it goes. Your upper, middle and lower back is filling with white light. Feel each muscle softening and your spine straightening and enjoying the relaxation.

The light is travelling into your upper stomach, dissolving tension and warming your abdomen, cleansing and relaxing your internal organs and the muscles of your lower stomach.

Relax and breathe deeply and send the light through your hips and buttocks, round into the pelvis and thighs.

Feel the light travel effortlessly into your legs, front and back, down into the knees, down your shins, calves and finally the ankles all the way to your feet, your toes and now your whole body is completely filled with white light.

Now you are full of light every particle of your body: bone, muscle, tissue, organs are filled with this healing light. Feel the peace.

Now send a beam of light from the base of your spine or from the soles of your feet deep into the earth. Watch the light spread like giant tree roots creating a strong foundation.

Ground your physical and energetic body to the Mother Earth.

Keep breathing deeply and bring your focus to your heart centre. Fill the middle of your chest entirely with light and watch as the light brightens and intensifies.

Now send the light outwards from your heart – outwards to your whole body and then through every pore of your skin in to your aura.

See this light spreading in front of you, below you, behind, above and either side. When your aura is full now concentrate and send this light outwards further and further, watch it dissolving any remaining unwanted energy from within and around you and when you feel clear imagine your positive intentions travelling out with this light into the universe, send love and healing outwards, express gratitude and feel at one with all.

When you feel a sense of peace, bring your light inwards to the confines of your aura again.

You are surrounded and absorbed in white light. Now choose a colour and place a shield a few inches thick around this bubble of light.

When you feel grounded, cleansed and shielded. Take a deep cleansing breath and bring your awareness back to the present moment and the room.

You will find that if you have trouble setting boundaries with people (saying no!); shielding is the first step in healing this issue. Many people believe they are being drained by demanding friends but in fact are draining themselves by holding resentful feelings and thoughts as they give in and help people when they do not want to but can't say 'no'. Resentment is a highly toxic and negative emotion, which wreaks havoc in your relationships and body. If you feel resentment then you are not really helping anyone and your emotions are letting you know its time to give to yourself.

Some people feel guilty about shielding as they worry that they are not giving as much as they 'should' or that they won't be able to feel empathy as deeply: Please do not feel guilty as guilt is toxic too and weakens your boundaries. When you are shielded, you can still give from the heart you are just not giving of yourself. When you are drained, tired or overworked you have less to give others.

Remember: The more (energy, money, fun, etc) you have, the more people you can help including your family and yourself!

Shielding colours

Choose whatever colour you like from the list or make up your own combination.

- White: Is divine light, it incorporates all colours. White light will protect you physically and psychically and can be used over possessions, animals, home, car and all things.

- Pink: Is the energy of love – the other person feels universal love without having to drain your energy.

- Bright/vivid green: Is healing for emotional and physical health conditions.

- Purple/Royal blue: Is great for psychic protection, healing and when you are with people who are angry, depressed or in very draining places, such as hospitals, pubs and shopping centres.

- Mirror: Surround yourself with a mirror to reflect all energy outwards but lower energies are always reflected back with love so that you are not sending out negative energy from yourself. Remember that everything that you send out is returned to you in a magnified way so you only want to be sending out love at all times!

- Metallic: When you just want to completely preserve your energy and to protect from very draining situations.

- Gold: Is very powerful and spiritual healing energy associated with healing deities such as Jesus.

- Chainmail: Imagine a chainmail shield over your aura to protect from any incoming energy. Thread together purple and gold for extra protection.

Use your imagination and make your own for example, titanium, or purple, gold and green together, experiment to see what works best for you.

When you shield and protect your energy, you will noticeably have more get up and go, and definitely feel less drained. Re-shield in harsh situations or when you notice yourself becoming tired.

Quick fixes for protecting your energy

When you suddenly realise you are being drained or feeling unprotected:

- Quickly think or say 'Shield'.

- Hold your hand over your solar plexus – this is your power centre. This method will prevent someone from plugging into your energy and overpowering, bullying or taking advantage of you either on the phone or in person.

- Ask for Archangel Michael. This powerful angel of light is the protector of the spiritual realm and he is more than happy to come instantly to your side whenever you ask. If you are feeling vulnerable, drained, unsafe in anyway, he can stand between you and other people to protect you and your energy.

- Deep breathing helps to clear and protect you.

- Cross your first two fingers and your legs at the ankles to create a closed circuit in your energy field.

- Imagine you are wearing a heavy velvet cloak with a hood; pull the cloak around and over your whole body to protect you. This works well when you are trying to disconnect from someone who is thinking about you a lot.

- The crystals: Amethyst, jasper and black tourmaline are protective gems that you can carry, wear or hold.

Chapter 6

The other side of the fence: Respecting people's energy

We all know how it feels to have our energy drained and the truth is that many of us have sat on the other side of the fence at times too. As a giver, it is far more likely that you try not to lean on others; the problem is that when we become low from over giving or overwhelmed with emotion and worry. We can to reach out to replenish or at least vent our frustration at someone.

Without healthy ways to manage our energy it is easy to drop the bundle on a caring friend or family member, or sometimes the first person that will listen. We are unconsciously dumping our toxins and perhaps even draining energy as we do this in our need to 'feel' better. Remember:

- Everyone is responsible for himself or herself and ultimately everyone can say no to unwanted requests or seek healthier ways to manage your energy.

- Be conscious of your own energetic behaviours and respect other people who may not be as aware.

- Establish firmer boundaries and shield your energy to help you to not take on so much – do not carry other people in an attempt to heal them.

- Learn to regularly clear, protect and ground your own energy.

- Seek out professional counsellors or healers to help you through difficult times.

- Write your feelings in a journal when you can't find anyone to listen.

- Take responsibility for all your words, thoughts and actions.

Energetic sticky beaks

Have you ever felt that certain people can see right through you, prodding at your mind or that they are undressing you with their eyes? That feels unpleasant and creepy doesn't it?

This is what it means to have bad energy manners.

These people are sometimes probing with their energy and thoughts and crossing our energetic boundaries. Sometimes we can actually feel this probe and react to it as if it is physical by backing off or folding our arms.

Someone does not even have to be present to affect us in this way — this is where strong shields can really help. Sometimes well meaning people can do something similar without intending to, especially if they want to heal or help a person. They reach out with a tentacle of their energy, sometimes without permission, to 'read' or heal another.

Energetically both of these examples can be like standing too close to someone or looking through their private possessions. It is like grabbing and raking through someone's handbag! Energy sensitive people can feel this and may back off. We need permission to energetically be close to someone as much as we would expect permission to physically be close! The trick is to know and teach safe polite ways of approaching others or reenergising rather than continuing the cycle.

It is good to remember is that your energy is very powerful and can behave like an extension of you, like a long arm reaching out, investigating its surrounds. Therefore, it's important to pull your energy in, so that people around you do not feel intruded upon.

A shielding visualisation to protect against probing energy

Sit or lie in a comfortable position and call upon Archangel Michael and your angels. Tell them that you would like to be protected completely from unwanted energy intrusions so that you can rest or concentrate. Tell them your thoughts and worries about energy intrusions.

Visualise your angels handing you a heavy velvet cloak, this cloak is beautifully soft and made of rich dark colours, the material shines, tiny flashes of light glimmer from all over it. Its lining is equally soft and smooth, cool to touch.

Put your arms through the long sleeves and pull the cloak over your shoulders, feel its soft heaviness over your body. Breathe deeply knowing that you are perfectly safe and protected by the powerful angels present. Pull the cloak around your body and tie its belt firmly, notice that it falls over your feet and covers your hands with its wide sleeves. Finally pull the soft hood up until its tip is almost touching your chin. You are now cocooned in this beautiful and soft cloak of protection. The material feels alive with light and your body responds to vibrating energy. All negativity and stress leave your being and you know that you are invisible to anyone with negative intent. You are safe and protected.

Use the cloak whenever you need a rest, a good night's sleep or if you are overwhelmed with outside energy. This cloak is a great protection when you feel that you are the subject of someone else's negative or unwanted thoughts. No one can reach you telepathically or energetically when you wear your cloak.

Ties

Ties are separate and different to the arms of energy that we send out. They are rope-like attachments made up of fear energy that keep us bonded to people, places, and things.
Conflict, jealousy, resentment, anger, addiction, insecurity and sadness are all examples of fear. Fear keeps us in a negative frame of mind and thinking about the past or future. Fear prevents people from enjoying their lives and their relationships. Ties negatively attach us to people and situations making it difficult to move on. Each time a fear thought is allowed, an energetic rope attaches to the source of the fear. This may be a person, a situation or even a place.

Love is the opposite to fear, as light is the opposite of darkness. Fear cannot destroy love but it can hide it as a cloud might hide the sun. In truth, divine love exists within every person and situation. All love is eternal even if the relationship does not continue or when a person passes over from this life. When I cut ties for clients they often worry that they are cutting the bond of love between themselves and the other person. This cannot happen; love bonds are eternal. Cutting the negative ties can actually allow the love to flow in a relationship; the release of negative emotion removes the 'clouds' that make loving relationships difficult.

This is good news for couples, families and friendships where conflict can be healed and the relationships can be renewed without the fear energy there to influence it.

Some people do not want to get closer to the person they have a tie to, for example, a past perpetrator, or someone that they recognise as being a negative force in their lives. They may fear that cutting the tie will invite this person into their life. Releasing a negative bond definitely does not mean that you have to reconcile, hug, say its okay and continue a relationship. In fact, cutting such ties makes it easier to move on as there will be no energy linking you together.

People often hold on to their negative bonds, as they perceive them to be a protection. They believe if they hold on to the anger or pain it stops a similar incident from occurring again. They might even believe it keeps them safe from an abuser to keep the incident fresh in their minds. The opposite is true. Through the Law of Attraction, like attracts like. Fear, anger or sadness in your energy can actually invite more of the same. The ties of fear also hold the person close in energy and the situation high in the mind so that it is difficult to move on to happier times.

The most common negative attachments are in relationships, although ties can attach to public figures, buildings, countries, addictions and even organisations. These ropes become thicker over time and if left unhealed can become like tree trunks of negative energy. Fear is draining and toxic, so of course an attachment will physically, psychically and emotionally affect the bearer. Every time you think of the situation negative energy will pass through the tie and vice versa.

Ties are the reason that people think, and talk about conflicts years after they have taken place. The negative charge that attached in the first place still exists and is triggered by fear. The most obvious example is of a person who was hurt by a relationship betrayal and years later cannot trust their new partner, or worse, will not even start a new relationship. They are afraid of love. They might desire romance and wonder why they can't meet their soul mate. The negative fear energy is activated whenever potential partners are around. Fear is the opposite of love, so love relationships can't survive in that atmosphere. The relationships break down, more ties of fear are created and the person moves on with the belief that they were correct to distrust. This person might have many ties, the thickest being to the first person who first hurt them.

Cutting ties is incredibly healing and very simple. It involves being willing to forgive and let go of the fear energy, recognising that it is having a damaging effect on all areas of life. Forgiveness means being ready to release the damaging emotions and thoughts in exchange for more positive and life affirming energy. It means you are ready to let go and live in the present moment rather than the past. It does not mean that you are happy that the incident happened or that you want to go back to the situation.
Forgiveness is truly a gift for the self – the other person does not even have to know that they are forgiven. You are releasing yourself from negativity so that more love and peace can enter your life.

Love can take on many forms other than romance. It can mean peace, health, happiness, abundance, flow and harmony. We all want these states and they mean different things for each of us. They are always there like the sun shining down on us the only thing that prevents us from receiving love is fear and cutting ties will release huge clouds of fear from your life.

Case study: Lesley*

Lesley came for an angel healing. She revealed that she had never forgiven her abusive father who was now deceased and that she still felt angry and upset when she thought of him. There was a huge tie from her heart and solar plexus to her father. She panicked when we tuned into this bond and another tie appeared at her throat making it hard for her to speak. This identified the fear that she felt of him and how it affected her in present day.

She found it hard to speak up when she was being bullied or pressured especially by males. She also found it hard to get close to her husband physically and emotionally. I called in Archangels Michael and Raphael and asked Lesley if she was willing to let this pain and fear go, telling her that she could be free just by being a little bit willing.

She nodded and I asked her to breathe very deeply and repeat in her mind 'that she was now willing to release all fear energy between her and her father'. As she did so, I asked Archangel Michael to cut the ties. He did so and the energy release was palpable. Lesley cried with emotion and relief as the Archangel Raphael filled her body with healing energy.

A few weeks later Lesley rang me to tell me she felt better and that she could even now think of her father without anger or fear. She even began to experience compassion toward him. Her relationships were improving as was her health and energy levels. This tie had been draining her life force energy for most of her life and she was now free.

* The name has been changed to protect their privacy

Ties like those Lesley experienced are filled with fear and pain and keep the person in a victim state.

Lesley had felt like a victim all her life. Her thoughts and beliefs around this subject attracted more negative experiences towards her through the undisputable Law of Attraction. In a few minutes and with some willing intention on her part, the angels were able to help Lesley release all that fear, releasing her from a prison of pain. The healing effect of tie cutting is like a wave that reaches all parts of the person's life including other family members.

The person on the other end of the tie receives the healing too – although for the client that is not necessarily important at the time. I believe this love and forgiveness has a ripple effect for the whole planet and for healing away pain in family lines into the past and future.

In a marriage situation or caring parent-child relationships, it is important that both parties receive the healing. A client can cut ties of resentment with their husband or wife and return home to find a more receptive loving partner. One client was concerned that her husband did not support her new spiritual interests; we cut ties with that fear. She returned home to find he had purchased an angel statue for her.

Case study: Tracy*

Tracy, a student of teaching, was having difficulties with a co-worker at the school where she works. This woman was acting out in anger towards students and teachers, often making them cry. This upset Tracy who used loving methods in her work, knowing how sensitive many children are. She was even thinking of leaving her job because of this situation.

During the Angel Psychic Healing session, the angels cleared ties of fear between Tracy and her co-worker. With the negative energy, safely removed, they then helped Tracy to see the divine truth of this woman and asked her to send positive energy towards her and not to buy into any ego-based drama or judgement thoughts. At the next session two weeks later Tracy reported that all the apparent negativity was healed and there were, no more problems and she would stay in her job!

* The name has been changed to protect their privacy

By cutting ties, you are in effect forgiving the past. Forgiveness is one of the highest vibrational and beautiful actions you can take for yourself and others. It will benefit you in so many ways because you are telling the angels and the divine source that you are willing to receive more love. This love will bring miracles!

Signs that you may have ties

- You are still angry and regularly talk or think about a past event or person that hurt you.

- You have a reoccurring localised pain that has not been identified with a medical reason, such as a lower back pain that worsens when you think or talk about a negative situation.

- You are drained or tired for no apparent reason.

- You become obsessed with mental scenarios about past conflicts.

- You are having trouble in your love life.

- You cannot move on from the past.

- You are having trouble selling a home, changing jobs, or any kind of change.

- You become angry for no particular reason with your partner or family members.

- You have an addiction to a substance or behaviour.

- You deal regularly with clients in a counselling, massage or other therapeutic position where people 'release' their pain.

How to cut ties

Archangel Michael with his powerful sword of light will effortlessly chop your ties and take them and all the associated energy to the light. You can only cut the bonds of fear and pain. The fine tethers of light that connect us to those we love are unbreakable. So never fear that you can cut a love tie. You actually enhance the love, if you wish between yourself and others when you release the negative energy.

Visualisation: Cutting ties

Sit or lie quietly and invoke your angels, the Archangel Michael and the Archangel Raphael and any other angels or divine beings that you would like to have present. I often ask for Jesus and

Mother Mary to assist with forgiveness and healing. Seal the room or area with white light and then tell the angels what your intentions are, for example:

Angels, Archangels Michael, Raphael and (any other spiritual guides) thank you for being here I now intend to cut any and all ties between myself and (name) I willingly release these ties and all the negative energy with in this relationship and my body, heart and mind.

Please help me to completely heal and forgive (name) I let go completely and I now invite more love and blessings into my life. Thank you for this healing, Amen.

Then take some deep breaths and relax.

Visualise or think of the other person. If this is difficult then imagine a symbol for the person, an old photograph or just their name. Place this person within a protective bubble of white light, I find this is useful for people who are reluctant to connect to the energy of the other individual.

Notice where the ties are on your body connecting you to the bubble/ person. Do not worry if you cannot see/ feel or sense these rope like attachments, it is not important. The most important thing is your intention.

Ask 'Archangel Michael I am now willing to cut these ties attaching me to (name) please take them to the light for healing.'

Breathe in and out deeply and allow Archangel Michael to cut through the attachments with his sword of light. As it cuts repeat 'I am now willing to release this.'

As the tie releases you may feel a pop in your ears, or a big sigh of relief, goose bumps or even a rush of emotion.

Keep breathing and allow Archangel Michael to completely clear you.

Visualise the bubble containing the person drifting away into the light until it becomes too small to see. This takes the energy.

Archangel Raphael will then come and send healing light into the area where the tie was attached. Breathe, relax and receive the healing. This light is immensely powerful and relaxing. If there is time, I find it useful to send the light right through the body and aura.

When you feel clear, shield yourself and thank the angels and guides for their help.

If you have difficultly releasing a tie, it may be because you still want to hold on to the anger or fear. As I mentioned before it could be because you believe that these emotions are serving you in someway. Remember all negative energy is toxic to your life and will not remain neatly filed away! It will seep into all areas: Your finances, career, health and relationships. You really do attract more abundance, love and peace when you release pain in this way. Ask yourself what do you want more of, love or fear? If you are experiencing difficulties, ask your angels to help you to feel more loving and peaceful. Below are some simple techniques to help you to release worry from your heart and mind.
It is also a good idea to imagine what life would be like without anger, fear and resentment. Most people long to be free of emotional pain and do not realise that a simple decision to be free is all it takes.

Releasing negativity and fear

Our mind hangs on to challenging situations and negative energy in the mistaken belief that worry will 'fix' a problem. This ego behaviour keeps us focussed on what is wrong. This standpoint makes it impossible to find creative solutions or attract healing or positive energy. The act of releasing a problem gives your angels permission to help you to heal or manifest a positive outcome. Just like a dog hanging onto its bone, the more you worry the tighter the problem hangs on. Letting go releases the issue to be transformed into a blessing. Releasing is an act of faith and trust. Handing over issues to God and your angels attracts speedy and creative solutions and miracles!

Releasing techniques

- Write down your feelings in a letter or journal page and burn it safely, and ask the angels to free you of all the negativity.

- Pray for the outcome to be for the highest good of all.

- Write down your fears about letting go or forgiving the issue and submerge them in a bucket of water. Visualise your problems and fear dissolving.

- Drop pebbles symbolising your feelings or the source of your worries into a river or ocean. (You can use this as a visualisation if necessary.)

- The Angel Box: Use a small box with a pretty exterior and call it your 'Angel' or 'Miracle' box. Keep a note pad and pen near your box. Each time you find yourself worrying or struggling, write a note to your angels asking for assistance. Tell them what you need help with and that you release the situation to them completely. Place the note inside the box and go do something to take your mind off your problem. Trust that the angels will work on this situation for you as you surrender worrying about it.

- Call in the Archangels Michael and Raphael and ask them to help you to release negative emotions.

- Visualise an angel carrying a sack or bag, breath deeply and as you do so imagine breathing out the negative emotions into the bag that he then takes away to the divine source.

- Imagine your angels dropping a basket in front of you. Place people, situations and emotions into this basket and watch the angels take away the basket. This is a good exercise to do before going to sleep at night.

- Imagine the source/s of your worries and stress stepping on to a train and waving them 'Goodbye'. Watch the train travel into the distance. Feel the relief in the knowledge that all of your concerns are being taken care of. This visualisation works when you want someone to move out of your life. Repeatedly visualise them going away to their destiny. Eventually this person will go of his or her own accord. Wish them love as they go and thank them for the lessons!

Managing resentment and psychic attack from other people

Psychic attack occurs when someone sends anger energy towards another. A sensitive person can feel this energy and it may even manifest as a physical pain usually in the shoulder or neck. It gives some truth to the phrases 'stabbing in the back', a 'pain in the neck' and a 'thorn in my side'. Be aware if you are using these phrases, as words are powerful, you do not want to manifest this energy! (You can undo such negative affirmations by saying 'undo' and then replacing it with a positive affirmation.)

Usually we are aware when someone is sending negative energy, such as after a painful relationship break up, an argument or because of jealousy. Gossip, slander, angry words and thoughts, cursing, spells and various forms of abusive sign language are all forms of psychic attack that can energetically impact the recipient. It is important to recognise our own role in the situation and withdraw all negative energy. It will exacerbate any problem to think vengeful or fearful thoughts or become overly worried about psychic attack. When you engage in such thoughts you actually weaken your energy field, which allows negative energy to penetrate.

Remember that your aim is to become clear and free of fear energy.

Revenge has highly negative consequences for the person who feels vengeful. Revenge, guilt, anger and resentment are all forms of fear and are low vibrating energy forms. They all indicate a need to release the surrounding thoughts and circumstances to God and the angels. Sending anything but love compassion and forgiveness creates negative karma. Remember that everything that you send out is returned to you threefold.

Those who send out negativity are coming from a place of fear and may not know better, as a sensitive person and after learning about energy you do know better. Instead of fostering anger, pray for healing and disconnect your energy from the situation. Cut your ties regularly.

As with all negative energy, the ideal angel to call upon is Archangel Michael, he can lift the daggers from your body and shield you. You can ask for a psychic dagger clearing when you cut your ties.

Healing yourself or others from psychic attack

- Seal your room and aura with white light and invoke the angels and guides that you wish to be present.

- Set your clear intention and tell them what you would like their help with.

- Say, 'Angels, Archangels and guides, please release me from all psychic daggers and dark energy of any kind from my body, energy, heart and mind. Please help me to send out forgiveness and compassion to the individuals who have sent me this energy and help them to find peace and happiness. I know that psychic attack is ego behaviour and does not come from the true person. Please take all negative energy to the light for healing. Thank you and amen.'

- Breathe deeply and allow the angels to lift the daggers and take them away. Feel the peace and release as they work on you.

- If you wish, visualise angels surrounding the person who seemed to hurt you. Disconnect your energy from them.

- Allow the Archangel Raphael to heal you with light.

- Now cover your energy with a purple shield to protect against further negativity.

- Thank the angels.

Protection against psychic attack

Visualise a pink, reflective shield surrounding you. Everything that hits this shield is immediately transformed into love and reflected back to the 'sender'. You can visualise this love as doves, pink bubbles or light. As the transformation occurs, the love is reflected outward to all who meet or think of you.

There is love at the centre of every person and situation, being able to see that love is powerful and life changing. Try this exercise if you feel you are clear of lower energy and willing to send love to someone who seems to be attacking you.

First call in your angels then use the visualisations in chapter five to ground and shield yourself.

Imagine accepting the attack in the form of a stone or energy and holding it in your hand, blowing on it and turning it into love, which triplicates in your hands. You can visualise this as spheres of pink or white light or another symbol of love such as roses.

Say, 'I accept this gift, thank you, I now transform it to love I send it back to you threefold.' Watch the love fly out from you and feel your heart opening.

A purple chainmail shield is a great protection against negative energy of any kind. Purple is the colour of Archangel Michael's energy and completely transmutes the pain and fear. The chainmail will prevent the daggers from lodging in your energy.

Ask an angel to be with you to catch and remove any daggers and take them to the light. See this angel in your mind, acting like a bodyguard or a Holy goalie!

How to prevent sending psychic attack

Yes, it is hard to admit but even a loving person has sent some less than pleasant energy to another. Sometimes it's just a habit of negative thought, sometimes encouraged by friends and colleagues or because you feel wronged. Apart from being against your sensitive nature, these actions can produce guilt. They carry a heavy price as the immutable Laws of Attraction and karma mean that what you send out is returned to you.

To avoid this ask your angels to help you to focus your words and thoughts only on love. They will act as a filter for you and you will immediately feel a bit off centre or some tightness in your body if you speak negatively. If you find yourself gossiping, bitching, and swearing or 'giving the bird' in traffic, then cancel it immediately and send out love instead – it is never too late!

It is a great idea to make a pact with friends to avoid negative conversations. Negative words affect your abundance, and create problems. Complaining weakens your energy and creates more of what you are complaining about. There are thousands of subjects to focus on other than the negative issues in life. What you focus on grows!

You might find that as a result of this change in attitude you no longer have anything in common with certain friends – this is normal and you shouldn't feel guilty just be aware that as your energy changes and lightens you will attract to you more positive energy in all its forms including new friends! Please remember not to moan about how negative your old friends were! Think or say, 'undo' or 'cancel that' and breathe out to clear the negative words and thoughts.

A note on swearing and cursing

I used to have mice in my home and as much as I love all animals, I became very frustrated with their chewing through food packets and leaving their little poos everywhere. I did not want to harm them and yet I was feeling stress. Every morning I would get up and wipe down the cupboards. As I cleaned, I would say something like, 'Darn you mice!' or jokingly quote the old cartoon, 'I hate meeces to peeces!'

I did not realise how negative I was behaving towards the mice. I was feeling victimised because I did not want to use poison and could not think of a kind solution. I was experiencing ego thoughts and feelings of irritation and stress. Then I began to find dead or dying mice all over the place yet still the mouse population grew! After praying for help, I realised that when I cursed the mice every morning I was actually sending out psychic attack energy, which resulted in harm for them. My negative focus on the mice was also creating more of what I was complaining about through the Law of Attraction: More mice!

This was a valuable lesson in the power of words and the Law of Attraction!

I began to pray to the angels and the diva of all mice to take the mice in a kind way from my home. I explained to the mice and the diva that I did not want mice in my home and that I wished them no harm but to find another warm home somewhere else. I asked for the best outcome for all. Within days there was not one mouse left and I never again had mice!

The effect of cursing on the little sensitive mice bodies was obvious. We do not immediately see the effect of cursing on a person. It gives me chills to think of how often children, partners, pets, government officials, politicians, traffic police and so on are cursed, even in jest. Remember we often curse inanimate objects such as computers and cars! Is it any wonder that these things sometimes break down on us? Everything is affected by the energy that we send out.

Instead of cursing, pray for the best outcome for all concerned, say affirmations and send blessings, then focus on what you want rather than what you do not want. Remember what you send out is returned to you.

Affirmations

Your thoughts, beliefs and spoken words are very powerful and they create real effects in the physical world. This is because they have energy; the whole universe is comprised of energy including your physical body. Your auric energy field acts in response to your thoughts, beliefs and words and you can change negative behaviours and outcomes by intentionally controlling your auric field. As you begin to feel happier, healthier and more vital, life improves. As you focus upon love rather than fear, you will attract loving situations towards you.

It makes perfect sense that affirmations spoken aloud and even thought powerfully attract wonderful situations and heal anything negative. Affirmations are positive statements about what you want, said in the present tense as if it has already occurred. You can use affirmations to heal a negative situation such as illness or debt; you can use them to attract something wonderful like a new car, a relationship or a job.

Affirmations work to raise your personal energetic vibration and magically align you with divine will. For example, if you declare several times a day 'My life is wonderful' then that becomes the truth for you. You will begin to attract positive situations, little miracles occur and the more irritating details of your life will start to clear up. Add visualisation to this and you can have some very powerful results; see your life flowing smoothly, see yourself receiving wonderful gifts and feeling healthy and energised.

Affirmations have successfully healed serious illnesses. Science is now showing how words and thoughts can have a dramatic effect on physiology, brain function and blood pressure. A Japanese scientist Dr Masaru Emoto (The hidden messages in water, New York, Atria Books, 2001), discovered that spoken, written and thought words affect water. In his experiments, water crystals changed according to the sentiment and intention of the words spoken to or taped upon water bottles. Hate filled expressions produced misshapen, deformed or non-existent crystals and love and gratitude created beautiful delicate shapes that seemed to express the sentiment of the words. There are amazing photographs in his books.

The human body is made mostly of water, as is our planet. In the same way as my cursing damaged the little mice so too will loving words heal you and your energy. The words you say and think make a huge difference to everything with in and around you, so think 'love' into all that you do and create beauty wherever you go.

To make positive affirmations for whatever you want in your life, start by writing down what you want in the long-term. For example, you may decide that you want to be happy, healthy, energised and to leave a job that you dislike and pay off debt. You do not want to mention anything negative in your affirmation. 'Pay off debt' is a negative affirmation. This creates a certain image that may trigger negative feelings inside of you.

Change the words to reflect how you want to feel and use phrases such as 'financial security', 'abundance' or 'prosperity'. Rewrite your desire and turn around negative statements. For example; 'I want to be happy, healthy, energised and to work in a job that I love. I want to earn a great income and easily be able to pay for all I need.'

A word of warning about negative statements. I have experienced that when people write their desires that include negative traits that they do not want, for instance 'I want a partner who is non-judgemental or I want a non-boring job'. It focuses the energy on what is not wanted, perhaps because there is a strong emotion connected to it. The universe will recreate the words with the strongest energy! So find positive words that describe your desires. For example 'a kind and loving partner' and 'adventurous and exciting work'.

Now your affirmation needs to be stated in the present tense as if it has already occurred. 'I want' states that you expect your desire to occur in the future, and focuses on the fact that you do not have it. 'I now have' states that you expect to have it. This dissolves feelings of 'lack'. Your energy, body and the universe responds to the vibration of what currently going on inside you. It does not matter whether you are thinking about the past or the future or even imagining a scenario, the Law of Attraction recreates the energy now and attracts a match to your vibration. The affirmation would now read 'I am happy, healthy and energised.

I now work in a job that I love, I earn a great income and easily pay for all that I need.' Repeat the two statements and notice how different each one feels within your body. Your energy changes and immediately uplifts your vibration. The changing vibration begins to immediately attract all that you affirm towards you and literally changes your inner and outer being!

Your affirmations become like a finely honed arrow sending your energy directly to what you want.

To make your affirmation more powerful you can add a visualisation or make a solid representation of your faith in its occurrence. For instance if you are waiting for good news, imagine how you will feel when your desire comes to fruition, see yourself smiling and telling friends. You could even design the celebration party invitation that you will use when the news comes.

The steps to making affirmations

- State your desires in a long hand non-edited sentence to get you started, so that you can really get in touch with what you want and do not want!

- Rewrite the sentence, taking out the negatives and turning them into positive statements.

- Now rewrite the sentence in the present as if it has already happened.

- Repeat the affirmation regularly throughout each day, silently, aloud, and as often as possible. Even if it does not feel true right now, it will increase in strength and power each time you express it as the truth.

- I suggest making one to three affirmations so that you do not overwhelm or scatter your energies, focus on how you want to feel and what you really want. Prioritise the affirmations and as you practice and begin to see the changes, you can then begin to attract more good things into your life.

Suggested affirmations

- I am happy, healthy and energised.
- I am beautiful.
- I am perfectly protected at all times.
- I only attract loving people and situations into my life.
- Life is fun.
- I am strong, sensitive and highly intuitive.
- I trust my intuition and my body.
- I know what is best for me.
- I am always powerfully guided and protected.
- I know what to do.
- I only speak loving words.
- All is well, I attract only good into my life.
- My life is wonderful in every way.
- I am loved.
- I am a role model for love and light.
- I now earn a great income.
- I happily accept all that is good into my life.
- I now work in a fulfilling job that is well paid.

- My love is powerful and healing to all that I meet.
- I trust my intuition and my angel's guidance.
- My body is healthy and vibrant.
- I love my body.

Chapter 7

Bringing it all together

Through the techniques described here, you have learned to clear, ground and protect yourself and bring your energy vibration into alignment with everything you want. You are now able to achieve clarity about what you do and do not want, and make great decisions. You own your energy and your power. You have started to walk your life path with confidence and purpose and attract abundance in the form of opportunities, people and items that are in alignment with what you want and your purpose.

You will have noticed that I have repeatedly mentioned forgiveness and a release of any negative emotions through out the book. Without doubt, negativity is the heaviest, most damaging toxin that a sensitive can encounter especially when it comes from inside your own mind. All of the practices and information offered are designed to return the body, mind and emotions to a state of love and to encourage self-responsibility and empowerment. No-one is ever a helpless victim, it can seem that way but there is always a choice, which begins with how you choose to see, think, speak and respond.

By honouring your sensitivity and managing your energy, you are making a difference to this world. Not only are you taking responsibility and being true to yourself. You offer others the opportunity to do the same by acting as a beautiful sensitive role model. Your courage and positive action will act as a shining light that will have a ripple effect throughout your whole life and into the lives of those that encounter you.

Thank you for being who you truly are and living in harmony with the earth.

Glossary

- **Acupuncture:** A therapeutic procedure that uses fine needles on energy points of the body to alleviate symptoms and pain.

- **Angel:** A non physical being that acts as a guardian, protector and messenger to humans, Angels are divine, loving and act only for the highest good of anyone who calls upon them. Angel means "messenger of God".

- **Angel Psychic Healing:** Angel Psychic Healing a very powerful healing modality that invites angels to the healing process. Angel Psychic Healing is the author's business and website name.

- **Ascended Masters:** Ascended Masters are powerful masters of spirituality, healing and knowledge who have died and become spiritual guides. They can be accessed through prayer and invocation to assist humanity.

- **Attraction, Law of:** The Law of Attraction is a principle that is said to govern humanity. The basis of the Law is that "like attracts like", therefore whatever you think, feel and speak about will be magnetically attracted into your life. When you control your thoughts and focus on positive situations and emotions you can improve your life.

- **Auditory psychic messages:** See Clairaudience.

- **Aura:** The energy field that surrounds and radiates from all living things. See Auric field.

- **Auric field:** A field of subtle, multicoloured radiations that surround all living things, including plants and animals, as a halo or bubble, these energies are described as electromagnetic forces. The aura contains information about the physical, emotional, mental, spiritual aspects of humans.

- **Authentic self:** The true essence of a person, also described as the higher self. The higher self is free of fear and negative emotions and always acts for the best good of yourself and others.

- **Bush flower essences:** A complimentary therapy derived from Australian native plants.

- **Clairaudient:** Clairaudience is the psychic ability that allows you to hear physical and non physical messages that are meaningful. A clairaudient may hear the voices of God, their angels, spirit guides and deceased loved ones. Psychic hearing also extends to the physical world where you may hear a song or words in the physical world that give you guidance!

- **Claircognisant:** Claircognisance means "clear knowing". A Claircognisant receives divine psychic messages into their mind. You might experience this as thoughts and ideas or as an instant knowledge about something or someone.

- **Clairsentient:** Clairsentience means "clear feeling" clairsentients are very sensitive to emotions and physical sensations. They receive psychic messages through their body and feelings. A clairsentient may be able to feel another person's back pain or sadness in their own body, OR will receive a certain feeling that for them will give them a message. For example a tight throat may mean they are not speaking their truth.

- **Clairvoyant:** Clairvoyance means "clear seeing". Psychic messages are received through visions and pictures in the mind's eye, detailed dreams or physical visions.

- **Clearing:** To clear the energy means to cleanse the body, emotions and aura of lower, negative and toxic energies using various methods including white light.

- **Colour therapy:** The seven colours of the spectrum are used to stimulate the body's healing processes.

- **Crown chakra:** the energy centre located at the top of the head, this chakra is "seen" as purple or white light and is concerned with spiritual connection. It is through this chakra that the God source energy is received.

- **Crystal children:** The crystal children are a group of children born in recent years that have certain characteristics such as large eyes, a crystalline or opalescent aura, very gentle and loving personality, a love of gems and rock crystals, and a high sensitivity. These children do not speak early on in their lives, preferring to use sign language and telepathy.

- **Crystal healing:** a healing modality using gems and crystals placed on or over the body with the intention to balance and clear the physical and energetic bodies.

- **Desensitised:** When a person "numbs" their physical and emotional and energetic awareness by consistently ignoring their normal physical and intuitive reactions. A person may override discomfort by downplaying their negative emotions or eating unhealthy foods.

- **Diva:** A Diva is a nature-being that is the overseeing angel of a particular area of the natural world. For all wild and domestic animals, plants, locations and oceans you can call upon the relevant diva or group of angels that oversees and protects that realm. For instance if you do not know the name of the angel or being that you want to pray to then ask for the mouse diva or the computer angels, the car angels or diva of your garden.

- **Earth angel:** Earth angel is a term given to a person who acts in loving ways for the good of humanity and the planet.

- **Earth-bound spirits:** Earth bound spirits are the spirits of deceased persons who remain on the earth plane and have not yet gone to the spiritual plane. They are kept here by their own fears such as guilt feelings, addictions, fears of judgement and punishment. There are many reasons that a spirit remains bound in this way, they are usually unhappy and require assistance to cross over.

- **Empathic:** To be empathic means to be able to sense the emotional and physical feelings of another within your own being.

- **Energetic being:** Your energetic being is the non physical part of you that includes your chakras, auric field and meridians. Your energetic being extends out from your physical body and can detect and absorb outside energy.

- **Energetic imprints:** An energetic imprint occurs when an intense and powerful event such as a trauma, battle or even regular prayers and healing have taken place in a certain location. This area will retain the emotion and energy of the event. The energy can be detected by sensitive people and the area may seem haunted or just feel strongly negative or positive.

- **Energy field:** See Auric field.

- **Entities:** Entity is a word used to describe an earth bound spirit or a strongly negative non human form of energy that has a separate distinct existence. Entities can derive from fearful thoughts that take on a life of their own.

- **Entrainment:** Entrainment is the synchronisation of energy vibrations to match another more dominant frequency.

- **Etheric field:** See Auric field.

- **Grounding:** Grounding is a method used to secure your

physical and energetic bodies to the earth. Grounding ensures that you are centred and living in the present moment.

- **Guidance system:** A name I have given to describe how your physical and emotional senses are constantly giving you information that you can use to guide your choices and life.

- **Guides:** Your guides are a spiritual team of loving beings including your angels, spiritual guides, and deceased loved ones who wish to guide and protect you during your life.

- **Healer:** A healer is one who works to bring about wholeness, health and wellbeing for humanity and animals.

- **Healing modalities:** Healing modalities are types of methods used by healers.

- **Higher self:** Your higher self is the part of you that is free of your ego and is connected to God / the universe.

- **Inbuilt receiver:** Your inbuilt receiver is the word I use to describe your senses. Your senses are receiving information constantly about you and your world.

- **Indigo children:** The Indigo generation are older than the Crystal Children and are defined by certain characteristics including sensitivity, an indigo coloured aura, high creativity, strong will and opinions about justice and environmentalism, a warrior type personality and leadership qualities.

- **Inner voice:** Your inner voice is the voice of your higher self or intuition. It is the part of you that wants your highest good in all things.

Intuition: Your intuition is your guide which talks through your senses and provides a strong feeling or knowingness. For instance "gut feelings".

- **Intuitive:** An intuitive is someone who uses their intuition regularly to give readings or guidance to others.

- **Karma:** Karma is a universal law of cause and effect. Karma is not punishment or reward for actions but rather the result of positive or negative thinking or actions. Negative karma can be adjusted by altering the cause which may be the negative or fear based thoughts.

- **Kinesiology:** Applied Kinesiology is an alternative healing modality created in 1976 which uses muscle testing to diagnose and give feedback on the functions of the body. Applied kinesiology draws together many other alternative therapies to treat any dysfunction.

- **Negative energy:** The energetic result of fearful thoughts and words.

- **Psychic:** Someone who can access information about people, places and situations using the senses of clairvoyance, clairsentience, clairaudience, claircognisance.

- **Psychic vampires:** a slang term for people who take life force energy from other people.

- **Solar plexus chakra:** the energy centre located above the naval which is concerned with personal power.

- **Spiritual healing:** Healing modalities that access God, Angels and spirit beings to heal and balance all life areas: physical, mental, emotional, spiritual and energetic.

- **Third eye chakra:** The energy centre located between the eyebrows, also called the brow chakra, this chakra is concerned with psychic vision and inner wisdom.

- **Toxins:** Toxins are substances or energies that are negative for the body, mind, spirit and emotions. Toxins can be from food, pollution, chemicals or from lower vibrating emotions and thoughts.

- Transmutation: Transmutation occurs when negative energy is taken from the person and sent away to be transformed into a more positive force.

- **True self:** See Higher self and Authentic self.

- **Universal kick up the butt:** A term I use to describe a painful life-changing event that comes as a result of ignoring intuitive guidance over a long period of time. The universal kick up the butt will force change upon the recipient having given her/him many opportunities to change their situation themselves. For example, when a person suffers an illness after years of unhealthy behaviours, or a person loses their job when they have had lots of guidance to change their work.

- **Visualisation techniques:** Visualisation techniques are creative mental images that can be evoked for healing, relaxation or goal setting.